WHEN YOUR CIRCUMSTANCES
CHALLENGE THE
PROMISES OF
GOD

THE MESSAGE OF
HABAKKUK

TIM ARMSTRONG

WHEN YOUR CIRCUMSTANCES CHALLENGE
THE PROMISES OF GOD: THE MESSAGE OF
HABAKKUK
Published in the United States by
The Chapel Publishing, Akron, OH

© 2015
ISBN: 978-0-9864429-4-0

Unless otherwise noted, Scripture used:
From the ESV® Bible (The Holy Bible,
English Standard Version®), copyright
2001 by Crossway, a publishing ministry
of Good News Publishers. Used by
permission. All rights reserved.

THE CHAPEL
PUBLISHING

TO HIM

Who redeems the righteous by faith

To my wife, Michelle

*Who continues to be the most Christ-like person I know.
Thank you for being my greatest encourager,
faithful partner, unending love.*

To the congregation of The Chapel

*These chapters were originally presented as sermons to
the congregation of The Chapel, Akron, in the fall of 2014
after shortly beginning my ministry with them.*

*Thank you for graciously learning and then applying
the truths we discovered together. You continue to be a
blessing to shepherd and pastor.*

TABLE OF CONTENTS

INTRODUCTION

I f a preacher steps up to a pulpit today and says, "Turn with me to the book of Habakkuk," chances are, most in the congregation would turn first to the Table of Contents.

I don't say this to embarrass anyone, but rather to illustrate a simple point: We aren't as familiar with some sections of our Bibles as we are with others. The Minor Prophets may well be the most unfamiliar books in all of Scripture.

We've probably arrived here honestly enough. The prophetic books are not as straightforward to read and understand as historical narrative and not as easy to "feel" as poetry. Some passages can be rather obscure and difficult to wrap your mind around. The prose can feel archaic with all its talk of kings, kingdoms, covenants, curses, warnings, and condemnation. What does any of that have to do with our life and times?

We may be tempted to leave those books to clergy and theologians. But I want to encourage you to take a fresh look.

Perhaps better than any other portion of Scripture, the prophetic books reveal that the people of Bible times were human beings just like you and me. In studying them, we discover that their lives, settings, and circumstances were more like our own than we'd ever imagined. As you make these discoveries, you'll come to appreciate that the prophetic books are tremendously rich and relevant to our life and times.

Join me in exploring the book of Habakkuk. One of the "Minor

Prophets" — the prophetic books are categorized as Major or Minor Prophets by length — Habakkuk is one of the shortest books of the Bible. It's also one of my favorites. When we're done, I think you will agree with me that it is one of the most practical books in all of Scripture. It tells us an ancient story that conveys a very modern and applicable message. Let me quickly brief you on that story.

It was some 600 years before the time of Christ when a prophet named Habakkuk stood in Jerusalem and pondered the state of his nation, Judah. He was shocked by what he saw. Everywhere he looked, evil was rampant; indifference toward God and even blatant idolatry thrived. And yet, God was silent. Where was He? How long would He allow this sinfulness to continue?

If that weren't bad enough, Habakkuk watched as another nation, Babylon, was closing in on Judah. The Babylonians were a war machine. They'd devoured every people who had stood in their path. Judah was next in line.

As he observed all of this, Habakkuk's sandals stood upon the fertile soil of the Promised Land. This was the very piece of ground that God had, long ago, promised to Abraham to be Israel's forever possession. That land represented their hope in God, as His chosen people. Now they were on the verge of being driven out by an enemy. It appeared that all hope was lost.

What do you do when your circumstances challenge the promises of God?

Where's the modern relevance?

There are situations and settings in our lives that set up just like this. No, you won't likely stand in the center of your town to see enemy armies approaching. But if you live any length of time in this world, you will experience a season that rocks you to your core.

Your telephone rings with the news … your boss calls you into the office … your doctor puts a hand on your shoulder … any number of scenarios can play out, and there you stand — as if all hope is lost.

What do you do when your circumstances challenge the promises of God?

Habakkuk's ancient setting becomes even more relevant the closer you look at it.

Some 2,500 years ago, his faith was tested in the face of a global power struggle and perilous times. Evil was around every corner —

Have you caught the news today?

Worries, woes, disease, genocide, terror, tragedy. Global struggle and perilous times — this is our world! What does it look like to have faith in such a world? How are believers to live? How are we to fulfill God's purposes amidst the chaos that is all around us?

When our circumstances overwhelm us, when God's promises seem unfulfilled, where do we turn? For starters, we long for answers: *Why, God? Where are you, God? How can you allow this to happen?*

Habakkuk asked those very questions. God answered him. The answers God gave weren't exactly the answers the prophet wanted to hear. But as the story unfolds, its message, that *the righteous shall live by faith*, is unmistakable.

That phrase, in fact, *the righteous shall live by faith*, probably looks familiar to you. Many consider it one of the most important verses in all of Scripture. It's found in the book of Habakkuk — and it's found right in the midst of a context where circumstances challenge the promises of God.

What we can learn from the book of Habakkuk will help us live by faith even when the wheels seem to be falling off our world, when life doesn't make sense. The lessons of Habakkuk provide insight into how God uses the present situations we find ourselves in — that can be confusing and even bewildering — to bring about His Kingdom plan in our lives and the lives of those around us.

We encounter a very basic contrast in Habakkuk — a prideful people are humbled, while the righteous live by faith. We see two pictures develop: one of unbelief and one of belief.

It's real. It's raw. It's a book of struggle, trying to come to grips with what God is doing. It invites us into the deep, dark questions of life, of wrestling with God's activities behind the scenes. Habakkuk's story reminds us that although God may seem silent or distant in our hardship, He's really at work in and through the situation we're experiencing, and that righteousness and justice *will* prevail.

These are incredibly relevant and applicable life lessons! Habakkuk is a book of hope!

In joining me on this journey, we're going to read through the whole book of Habakkuk, giving it a verse-by-verse consideration. It will be best for you to have your Bible open, too. Be like the Bereans who were noted "for their eagerness in examining the Scriptures daily to see if those things were true" (Acts 17:11). In other words, don't just take my word for it — turn to the Word. Let Scripture be its own commentary. As you search things out, striving to understand and apply the truth Habakkuk has to teach, I will be honored to lead and encourage you along the way.

It's not as imposing as you might think. Habakkuk is unique among the prophetic books because it feels more like reading someone's journal than it does prophetic oratory. It provides us one of the most remarkable sections in all of Scripture, as it contains an extended dialogue between the prophet Habakkuk and God.

The book is laid out like this:

- (1:1-4) Habakkuk complains about the sins of the people, the evils and injustice that he sees. He initiated a conversation with God because he wanted to see God do something more.

- (1:5-11) God answers, though it is not what Habakkuk wanted to hear. God is sending the evil Babylonians to "cure" Judah.

- (1:12-2:1) God's shocking answer prompts a second complaint from the prophet. Now he asks moral questions: "Are you good, God?"

- (2:2-20) God answers again, saying essentially, "Just as you began with me by faith, now you must live by that faith."

- (3:1-19) Habakkuk prays a confession of trust and even joy in God. This is one of the most beautiful — and relevant — prayers recorded in the Bible.

What do you do when your circumstances challenge the promises of God? You start by familiarizing yourself with the message of Habakkuk.

This wonderful little book begins with a believer, much like you and me, struggling to find God within the circumstances surrounding him. It ends with that same man of God reassured and resting anew in God's promises.

Isn't *that* where we want to be? Let's retrace his journey....

1

Who's In Charge?

Several years ago, I received a phone call that a friend of mine was in the emergency room — he was coaching soccer and experienced some chest pains. I fully expected that when I entered the room, he would be seated there with a nurse or two, covered in wires. I thought they'd be running tests on his heart.

But I walked into an entirely different scene. My friend was laying flat on the table. He wasn't moving. Doctors and nurses were frantically at work. One was doing chest compressions — the situation was desperate. My friend's wife stood beside him, stunned. Their children huddled just behind her. When I stepped into the room, the head physician locked eyes with mine, and I knew, without a word, he was gone.

I put my hand on his wife's shoulder. She looked at me and spoke just one word, "Why?"

In the days and weeks that followed, that question would torment her. Forty-two years old; fit; young family; young wife; plans, goals, a bright future ahead of them all — "Why?"

It is a question that we have all asked at one time or another: The unexpected death of a loved one — "Why?" A sudden loss of employment — "Why?" A relationship that seemed rock-solid falls apart — "Why?" Another miscarriage — "Why?" A diagnosis that leaves you reeling — "Why?" Violence, abuse, betrayal, sorrow, disappointment, injuries, crime — "Why?"

It's not a new question.

Some 2,500 years ago the prophet Habakkuk was so disturbed by what was happening around him, he cried out to God and asked, "Why?" But he not only asked the question, he got answers. Habakkuk's dialogue with God is recorded in the Bible, in the book that bears his name. It's an ancient book that is very modern in its dealings.

Some Historical Context

A quick review of Old Testament history will help set the stage. There was a time in Israel's history when the kingdom was united under the rule of King David, and then his son Solomon. When Solomon died, things deteriorated. Rehoboam, Solomon's son, was crowned king, but the 10 northern tribes of Israel rebelled against him. They followed Jeroboam as their king. The kingdom divided — Israel in the north and Judah in the south. There's likely a map in the back of your Bible that depicts that era of history.

The Northern Kingdom was conquered in 722 BC by Assyria. The books of 2 Kings and 2 Chronicles, as well as the prophetic ministries of Elijah, Elisha, Jonah, Amos, and Hosea, give us a great deal of that story.

The Assyrians then set their sights on the Southern Kingdom. God intervened. You may recall the account Isaiah provided — "an angel of the Lord went out and struck down 185,000 in the camp of the Assyrians" (Isaiah 37:36).

One hundred and thirty-six years later, in 586 BC, the Southern Kingdom was conquered by Babylon. 2 Kings and 2 Chronicles record the history. The prophets who ministered to the Southern Kingdom and surrounding its fall are broken up by scholars into two groups — pre-exilic and exilic — or, in other words, those who prophesied before the exile of the Jews to Babylon and those who ministered during and after.

Habakkuk was a pre-exilic prophet. We really don't know much about the man, other than the fact that he was a contemporary of Jeremiah, Nahum, and Zephaniah. We do know his place in history. Scholars have fixed the time of his ministry between 612 and 586 BC. That's important to know, because *when* he wrote makes all the difference in the world.

Habakkuk ministered during 25 of the most tumultuous years of Judah's history. They started with the death of King Josiah — known for the sweeping religious reforms he implemented. He's introduced in the Bible this way:

"Josiah was eight years old when he began to reign, and he reigned thirty-one years in Jerusalem. And he did what was right in the eyes of the Lord, and walked in the ways of David his father; and he did not turn aside to the right hand or to the left" (2 Chronicles 34:1-2).

Please don't miss the phrase "he did right in the eyes of the Lord" in Josiah's introduction. Judah had been led by one evil king after another — Josiah's grandfather, Manasseh, among the worst of them, leading the people into idolatry. Josiah set out to bring reform.

> "For in the eighth year of his reign, while he was yet a boy, he began to seek the God of David his father, and in the twelfth year he began to purge Judah and Jerusalem of the high places, the Asherim, and the carved and the metal images" (34:3).

At 16 years of age, Josiah began an aggressive campaign to rid Judah of pagan altars and images, many of which were erected under the leadership of his father and grandfather.

> "And they chopped down the altars of the Baals in his presence, and he cut down the incense altars that stood above them. And he broke in pieces the Asherim and the carved and the metal images, and he made dust of them and scattered it over the graves of those who had sacrificed to them" (34:4).

Authentic faith was being restored! What a day it must have been for those who followed Yahweh, the God of Israel! But Judah didn't exist in a vacuum. The rest of the world didn't stop to take notice. While Josiah was leading Judah's renewal, three world powers were vying for supremacy around them — Babylon in the south, Samaria in the north, Egypt to the west. Judah was situated right in the middle of it all.

As the three powers went to war, Judah was drawn into the

conflict. Josiah, their king, was killed. The tragedy sent Judah reeling into turmoil and a rapid spiritual decline.

Use your imagination for a moment. Imagine your country, the backdrop of its stability and security, gone! Imagine your country's economy, in an instant, upside down! Imagine your nation's political standing in the world, poof! Imagine the moral and religious fiber of your society, shattered! That describes Judah in the day Habakkuk ministered. How would you feel?

A ruthless enemy was sweeping the land — Judah was in its path — and Habakkuk turned to God and asked, "Why?"

This is Habakkuk's backstory. This is where we find an ancient prophet with a modern message. If you were to launch into this book without any knowledge of the setting, you'd be left scratching your head, wondering, "Why is this even in the Bible?" But armed with the history, you're able to read Habakkuk's longings, and relate. Spend time in this book, and it will help answer the most profound question we ask — "Why?"

God, Are You Listening?

One danger I hope you avoid when reading the Bible is getting lulled to blasé by the black and white on the page — to read emotionally charged passages as if you're reading a dictionary. Just words. When you read the opening verses of Habakkuk, please don't hear it in some flat-line, monotone voice. When the prophet begins, "Why, Lord?" it's with the same emotional heartache, longing, and confusion as the young widow in the ER. Read this passage that way:

"O Lord, how long shall I cry for help, and you will not

17

hear? Or cry to you 'Violence!' and you will not save? Why do you make me see iniquity, and why do you idly look at wrong? Destruction and violence are before me; strife and contention arise. So the law is paralyzed, and justice never goes forth. For the wicked surround the righteous; so justice goes forth perverted" (Habakkuk 1:2-4).

Do you see what the prophet is saying? Can you feel it? He's pleading, "Where are you, God? I've been crying out and you're not hearing me! Why, Lord? Why? Why don't you come and do something? Are you listening to me?"

It's bold. It's honest. You may even read this and think, "I can't imagine talking to God that way." If that's the case, one practice you should adopt is regularly reading through the Psalms. In the Psalms you'll find the pathos of the Scriptures — the poignant, the tragedy, the sadness — genuine and authentic heart-cries are found there. Consider this example:

"How long, O Lord? Will you forget me forever? How long will you hide your face from me? How long must I take counsel in my soul and have sorrow in my heart all the day? How long shall my enemy be exalted over me?" (Psalm 13:1-2).

That's the spirit in which Habakkuk cried out. It seemed to him that God had been indifferent to his pleas. It seemed to him that God was being mocked — righteousness was failing; the wicked were triumphant. "Are you seeing this, God?"

Habakkuk had nowhere else to turn. His country was in ruins. His countrymen were being slaughtered. He had nothing else to do but storm the throne of God, demanding, "How? Why? Don't you see this? Are you going to answer me?"

That's exactly what God does. He answers:

> "Look among the nations, and see; wonder and be astounded.
> For I am doing a work in your days that you would not believe
> if told" (1:5).

Well, that much sounds pretty good. This is the way we'd hope God would respond to our plea — "Yes, I hear you, and you're going to be astounded at what I'm about to do!"

Amen! Bring it on! But God continued, and His answer didn't unfold the way Habakkuk had hoped or expected.

> "For behold, I am raising up the Chaldeans, that bitter and
> hasty nation, who march through the breadth of the earth, to
> seize dwellings not their own" (1:6).

At this, the prophet's heart must have fallen. Do you know who the Chaldeans are? They're the Babylonians. They're the enemy oppressing Judah, slaughtering her citizens. God's answer had to have been a bombshell to Habakkuk:

"Lord, we're being attacked!"

"Yes, I know. I'm raising up the attacker."

God described them as a "bitter and hasty nation" on the march, conquering lands not their own. Habakkuk and those of his day observed it with their own eyes. And they saw themselves as next in Babylon's path. God continued describing the oppressor, it could only have added to Habakkuk's angst:

"They're dreaded and fearsome" (1:7). "Their horses are swifter than leopards and more fierce than evening wolves" (1:8). "They come for violence … they gather captives like sand" (1:9). "At kings they scoff … they laugh at every fortress, for they pile up earth and take it" (1:10). "They're guilty men whose own might is their god" (1:11).

Are you sensing any comfort yet? Any "Gee, God, I'm glad we've had this little chat"? What graphic images! What terror! When God began, "You're not going to believe what I'm doing," He was right. Habakkuk couldn't believe it.

The cure sounded worse than the disease. How could a holy God do this? Habakkuk addresses that in his second complaint:

"Are you not from everlasting, O Lord my God, my Holy One? We shall not die.
O Lord, you have ordained them as a judgment, and you, O Rock, have established them for reproof. You who are of purer eyes than to see evil and cannot look at wrong, why do you idly look at traitors and remain silent when the wicked swallows up the man more righteous than he?" (1:12-13)

Those words reveal a lot about Habakkuk's heart at the moment, and its despair. "Are you not the everlasting God?" And more specifically, "*My* God, *my* Holy One?" In the phrase "we shall not die," the prophet framed this whole experience in the truth he holds deeply — God is a covenant-keeping God. There must be a redeeming point to all of this, although he can't fathom it.

Then comes the question again: "Why?" Habakkuk knows God

to be so pure that His eyes cannot even look upon evil — so how could He possibly be wielding it? "Why do you idly stand by? Why do you remain silent? Why, God?"

> "You make mankind like the fish of the sea, like crawling things that have no ruler. He brings all of them up with a hook; he drags them out with his net; he gathers them in his dragnet; so he rejoices and is glad. Therefore he sacrifices to his net and makes offerings to his dragnet; for by them he lives in luxury, and his food is rich" (1:14-16).

If you substitute the word *Judah* for *mankind*, Habakkuk understood that it was God who had made His people like defenseless fish to be caught up in Babylon's net. The "he" in these verses refers to the wicked foe — Babylon was catching up all the peoples in their path, with revelry and rejoicing, praising their war machine.

> "Is he then to keep on emptying his net and mercilessly killing nations forever?" (1:17)

Is this going to go on right underneath your nose, God? How long? Why?

God has not yet given Habakkuk a definitive answer. Have you noticed that? Heaven is silent. Have you ever been there before? Have you ever wondered, "How long am I going to have to deal with this, God? When will you hear me? How long must I cry out to you? How many times must I ask? Why?"

First Things First

Habakkuk chapter 1 ends right there. You might be thinking, "What in the world can I learn from that?" But this is only the beginning of the story; it's only the beginning of our study. There are some foundational principles for us to gather, here, before we move on. Without this groundwork, you won't be prepared for how God specifically answers Habakkuk's pleas. And without these foundational principles, you won't be prepared for how God answers you, when you cry out asking, "Why, Lord?"

The first principle is this: God is in control. It's ironic, because from Habakkuk's perspective it looked as if God was out of control — remember, in those first four verses, he was in disbelief and asked, "Are you seeing this?"

HEBREW WORD HELPS

For I am doing a *work* in your days that you would not believe if told (Hab. 1:5).

Original Word: פֹּעַל
Part of Speech: Noun Masc.
Transliteration: poal
Phonetic Spelling: (po'-al)
Definition: doing, deed, work

In this context: *An approaching work of God; a work accomplished by God*

God's answer affirmed, not only was He seeing it, He was in control right down to the details, "For I am doing a work in your days." The Hebrew word translated "work" in verse 5 means "something accomplished by another." God took responsibility for what was going on. He was at work.

God is often the one who does the work. Do you remember the apostle Paul's perspective on God's work in our lives? It's a great passage that reminds us who's in charge:

> "And I am sure of this, that he who began a good work in you will bring it to completion at the day of Jesus Christ" (Philippians 1:6).

Here, too, the Greek word rendered "work" refers to work that is the result of another. It's not your work. It has never been your work. It's God's work — and what's the promise? He's started a work in you, and He will bring it to completion in Christ. You many not know what's happening. You might not understand the circumstances you're in. But God does. He's in control. He's doing a work.

That's exactly what He says to Habakkuk. "Habakkuk, I am doing a work. I'm in control. I'm moving things forward." It may seem like utter chaos, but a foundational principle to grasp: God is in control, right down to the details.

Have you discovered this in your own life?

It really doesn't take long. It doesn't take much living before you realize you don't have a lot of control over anything. Who can you rely on? The One who says, "I am in control, I'm doing a work in your life."

That brings us to a second principle: The details aren't random, but they're part of His divine plan — they're part of a bigger picture. Remember that Habakkuk was a contemporary of the prophet Jeremiah. You may be familiar with this passage from Jeremiah, written about the same time as Habakkuk:

"For I know the plans I have for you, declares the Lord, plans for welfare and not for evil, to give you a future and a hope" (Jeremiah 29:11).

Jeremiah saw the same terror coming. Speaking to the people of Judah on behalf of the Lord, he assured them that God held them — and their future — in His hands. Reading that God has plans for us in English is tremendously encouraging, but the Hebrew word rendered "plans" is even richer; it speaks of an idea or thought, God's

GREEK WORD HELPS

And I am sure of this, that he who began a good *work* in you will bring it to completion at the day of Jesus Christ (Phil. 1:6).

Original Word: ἔργον, ου, τό
Part of Speech: Noun, Neuter
Transliteration: ergon
Phonetic Spelling: (er'-gon)
Definition: work, employment; a deed, action; that which is wrought or made, a work.

In this context: *work which is made or wrought in you*

ideal purpose. It carries the weight, "I am in control, and I have a plan. I have the outcome in view."

What does that tell you about your God? If He has a plan, could His plan include my annihilation? That must be what Habakkuk was thinking. Does His plan include crushing my life emotionally? The absence of any security? Does it include my decimation?

No! "I know the plans I have for you, declares the Lord … for welfare and not for evil … a future and a hope."

You've heard that great passage, Romans 8:28, which says, "We know that for those who love God, *some things* work together for good." Of course that's not what it says! It says "All things!" *All things* absolutely include those moments when you're asking, "Why?" All things! It certainly includes moments of utter despair when you can't make sense of it, and when you can't see the future. *All things!*

The third principle flows from the first two. If God is in control down to the very details, and if He has a divine plan, then God has a divine reason for why He does what He does.

You remember that Habakkuk began his second complaint by asking, "Are you not from everlasting?" In the same verse he said, "You have ordained [these things we're going through] as judgments." It's as if God said, "You need to see this as coming from me." Habakkuk did. I cannot overstate the importance of that concept for us.

I had a professor in seminary that often warned his students: "You are only one phone call away from tragedy." Think about that. It is so very true. It could happen that as you're reading these words, your telephone rings — one call can change the trajectory of your life.

A week before I graduated from seminary I received a phone call from my mother. She wasted no time with greetings or pleasantries; she just said, "Your father is dead." They were out shopping. My father, a blue-collar worker, had never really owned a suit. They'd bought a suit for him to wear to my graduation — a week later we buried him in it.

Five years later, I received another phone call like that from my mother. Those terrifying words: "I have cancer." It was right during one of the busiest times of my life. We were starting a church, raising a young family, trying to make ends meet, back in my hometown — and with my father gone I was expected to be there. A short time later, my mother was gone.

Outwardly, I must have been as blank and sterile as I was feeling on the inside. At one point, my wife asked, "What is the matter with you? What has happened?" It was, perhaps, the first time in my life that I really opened up to her; tears started to flow, and I couldn't turn them off. The best way I can describe the moment is that I was just broken — broken and I couldn't repair it. I couldn't come to terms with it.

I share this with you because I've realized that this is a road each of us will walk, sooner or later. We become broken. We turn to God. We turn to pastors and counselors. We seek help. I had always thought it was a sign of weakness to go to a professional for help, but I was wrong. It's the best thing you can do! You don't have trouble going to a doctor to fix a sore throat, do you? Why is that any different than seeing a professional about fixing the inside of you?

I determined, "I'm going to go see someone who will help me." In one of those counseling sessions, this Christian man said to me, "You have to see this as coming from your Heavenly Father. He has a divine plan — He has a reason."

You initially rebel at that thought. You want to scream, "God, you are not like that! I don't want to think of you as that kind of a

God, who would put me through such pain!" But He has a divine reason. What is He trying to accomplish in us? He's trying to make us more like Jesus.

This is the same God who watched His Son crippled on a cross — allowed the pain. You see, He leads us through these dark valleys, not to leave us there, not to crush us, not that we would live a life of despair or hopelessness. But He leads us through these valleys so that we might understand we have a merciful, loving God who will move us through the most difficult things in life to put us exactly where He wants us to be.

When you come out of these times, what happens? What was once broken and crushed inside of you springs anew. You have a greater capacity to love God and a greater capacity to love others who are moving through similar circumstances and experiences.

God brought Habakkuk to the point of breaking. He brought Judah to the breaking point. What does Habakkuk do? He addresses

HEBREW WORD HELPS

For I know the *plans* I have for you, declares the Lord, *plans* for welfare and not for evil, to give you a future and a hope (Jer. 29:11).

Original Word: מַחֲשָׁבָה
Part of Speech: Noun Fem.
Transliteration: machashabah
Phonetic Spelling: (makh-ash-aw-baw')
Definition: thoughts, purposes

In this context: *God's ideal purpose*

God in verse 12, "O LORD," — he used the covenant name Yahweh, right-sizing God in his own mind. Later in the same verse, "O Rock." He declares: God is his foundation stone.

God is often referred to as the Rock in the Old Testament. You've heard it many times:

> "There is none holy like the Lord: for there is none besides you; there is no rock like our God" (1 Samuel 2:2).

> "The Lord is my rock and my fortress and my deliverer, my God, my rock, in whom I take refuge, my shield, and the horn of my salvation, my stronghold" (Psalm 18:2).

> "Let the words of my mouth and the meditation of my heart be acceptable in your sight, O Lord, my rock and my redeemer" (Psalm 19:14).

In these moments of absolute brokenness and bewilderment, this is what we have to do — we have to right-size God in our minds. My Rock! God is in control. Down to the details, it's part of His divine plan. And He has a divine reason.

The fourth principle: God has a divine timetable. It's not by chance that it's happening now. The confluence of all that is going on in your life — it's not coincidence. Events in our lives are unfolding on God's divine timetable.

Recall the very beginning of God's answer to Habakkuk. He began: "Look among the nations and see; wonder and be astounded. For I am doing a work" — don't miss the next three words — "*in your days* that you would not believe if told."

It's not by chance that you're going through these things now — God is at work *in your days*. It's not before, it's not after, but it is unfolding in precisely the timing He has determined.

Ready As We Can Be

Through the first chapter, God hasn't specifically answered the prophet yet, but He's prepared him, given him a solid foundation on which to stand. He's assured Habakkuk: I am in control. I have a divine plan. I have a divine reason. I have a divine timetable. Stand on these principles — because I'm going to answer you.

You and I can make this personal. Just add the words "in my life" to the end of each of those principles. God is in control in my life. God has a divine plan in my life. God has a divine reason in my life. God has a divine timetable in my life.

These are foundational pillars that prepare us to move through the rest of Habakkuk, and prepare us for God's answer to our own question, "Why?"

Does God answer Habakkuk specifically? He does. Are you ready to turn the page?

2

Where To Go When Things Go Wrong?

T he book of Habakkuk opens with what we might consider a volcanic complaint by the prophet, repeatedly asking the question, "Why?"

Judah had been in the midst of glorious spiritual reforms under King Josiah when they were drawn into war, and their beloved king was killed. With his death, the nation began to deteriorate into ruins — economically, politically, morally. The feared Babylonians, that great and evil adversary, stood poised to sweep through Judah and take the people captive.

Habakkuk exemplifies great faith and a high concept of God — we saw that in the language of his complaints — but he is absolutely perplexed because things are not taking the course he expected. He had been asking God for national revival. What he was getting was national captivity! He watched it all unfold — in disbelief.

To wrap your mind around this, imagine praying to God with

great pathos, great passion, that He would begin to turn our nation back to its Judeo-Christian foundation. Imagine praying that there would be sweeping revival through the economic, political, and social systems of our country. Imagine that God answered you, but the answer wasn't what you expected: "I'm going to change your country by allowing an Islamic takeover." You'd pray, "God, that's not what I was asking for!" That's what was going on in Habakkuk's world.

Moral Questions

So far we've gathered four foundational principles upon which to stand when it seems like the wheels are falling off of our world: God is in control in my life. God has a divine plan in my life. God has a divine reason in my life. God has a divine timetable in my life. Commit these to memory and you're ready to move forward in the book of Habakkuk.

But before we do, let's be honest: you can know those principles, have them memorized, and believe in them, yet that doesn't mean they're easy to practice.

The reality here is that when these types of events occur in our lives, we start asking the moral question, "God, are you fair?" Conflict rises within us. Is God fair? Is He just? Is God good? If He is, how could He let this happen?

If we're honest, it's more often than not that we are confronted with these questions. You see some type of natural disaster change the landscape of a third-world country; you see all of these people displaced; you see children homeless, orphaned; people who already had little now have absolutely nothing — what do you say? You say, "God is this fair? Is this right? I thought you were a good God! How can you allow it?"

When we see abuse, we cry out, "God, are you aware of what's going on here?" Human trafficking, for instance: A few years ago I was in Cambodia, and I saw what looked like a businessman walking down the street, and he had on his arms two Cambodian girls. They couldn't have been much more than 11 or 12 years old — prostitutes. They're in a horrible situation, they're locked in and they can't get out, and you think, "God, where are you? What's going on? How can a good God stand idly by?"

Let's not be afraid to approach the tough moral questions. Habakkuk wasn't. He met them head on. You remember when the prophet began his second complaint:

"You who are of purer eyes than to see evil and cannot look at wrong, why do you idly look at traitors and remain silent when the wicked swallows up the man more righteous than he?" (Habakkuk 1:13)

He's asking the moral question: "How can you? Is this right? Is this just?"

How do you move forward when you're faced with such troubling questions? Some don't. Some, even though they know the foundational principles to stand on, withdraw. They drop out, move away from God, and move away from His Church. They become bitter or angry with Him. Do you know anyone like that? Have you ever been there?

What is the way forward from here? Again, Habakkuk becomes our teacher. He teaches us valuable lessons for following God through seasons of great uncertainty. In the first verse of the second chapter,

Habakkuk gives us some very practical, relevant help in how to face the moral questions like, "Why? Is God fair? Is He just in allowing these things?" It reads:

"I will take my stand at my watch post and station myself on the tower, and look out to see what he will say to me, and what I will answer concerning my complaint" (2:1).

Chapter-and-verse divisions in our Bibles are helpful — they help us find things. But they're not a part of the original writings. Editors added them in later. Occasionally, they divide something that maybe shouldn't have been divided. That's the case here. Notice that this verse really is a continuation of Habakkuk's words from chapter 1. At the end of all those very tough questions, he concluded: "I will take my stand at my watch tower."

The Way Forward

In this one sentence, Habakkuk shows us where to go when things go wrong. In fact, he gives us four specific steps to take. To help you see them clearly and to remember them, I'll outline them with help from the letter "R" — four words: *Retreat, Remind, Rethink* and *Recommit.*

How do you move forward? The first step is Retreat! That sounds funny, because when you think of *retreat* it tends to be in a military sense, withdrawing in defeat. That's not what we're talking about. *Retreat* can also be understood in a spiritual sense — perhaps you've been on a retreat, withdrawing to a quiet or secluded space, stepping away for a time to meditate, to contemplate.

HEBREW WORD HELPS

I will take my stand at my *watchpost* and station myself on the tower, and look out to see what he will say to me, and what I will answer concerning my complaint (Hab. 2:1).

Original Word: מָצוֹר
Part of Speech: Noun Masc.
Transliteration: matsor
Phonetic Spelling: (maw-tsore')
Definition: siege enclosure

In this context: *A platform for watch*

Habakkuk began, "I will take my stand at my watch post." He's not talking about this metaphorically. He's referring to an actual place. The Hebrew word rendered "watch post" refers to an observation tower or stronghold. The concept was well known — they were a familiar sight in Habakkuk's day, a place where a guard would go to watch over a field or vineyard. In the midst of asking "Why?" and wrestling with the tough moral questions, Habakkuk retreated to a sacred place. He determined to crawl up into a watch tower and, there, wait upon the Lord. He retreats to a quiet place.

That reveals much wisdom for you and me: When we're in the midst of wrestling with deep questions in our lives, we shouldn't just plow forward. That's the tendency, though — to push on, attempting to push through. But it's not the best course to take. It would be better to take a step back and retreat to a sacred location like Habakkuk.

Maybe you have such a place in your life. Perhaps it's a spot within your home that you go when you seek after God. Maybe it's your car during your commute — the radio turned off, or on, for that matter. After all, it's *your* sacred space.

Maybe it's a walk in the wilderness. Maybe it's the mall — my teenage daughters think that's a sacred place. Habakkuk had his. Where's yours?

Once you've retreated to that sacred place, what do you do there? You wait. I'm not really keen on waiting. Chances are you aren't either. We live in a society that's not very good at it. But one thing you find in Scripture, over and over, is that a regular component of our relationship with God is that we must wait on Him. Consider a few examples from the Psalms:

"Be strong, and let your heart take courage, all you who wait for the Lord!" (Psalm 31:24)

"Our soul waits for the Lord; he is our help and our shield" (Psalm 33:20).

"Be still before the Lord and wait patiently for him" (Psalm 37:7).

Why is waiting so integral to our relationship with the Lord? There is residual benefit in waiting. While we wait, God is accomplishing something in us. The prophet Isaiah had this to say:

"But they who wait for the Lord shall renew their strength; they shall mount up with wings like eagles; they shall run and not be weary; they shall walk and not faint" (Isaiah 40:31).

Take a look at Psalm 27. It's author, King David, starts by asserting his confidence in God and his desire to be in God's presence. But from there he laments the extreme difficulties he's experiencing at the moment. In the middle of the passage, he becomes brutally honest: he feels as if God is hiding His face, has turned away. But he isn't letting up. He's waiting — he's actively waiting. Look for each of those steps in David's sonnet:

"The Lord is my light and my salvation; whom shall I fear? The Lord is the stronghold of my life; of whom shall I be afraid? When evildoers assail me to eat up my flesh, my adversaries and foes, it is they who stumble and fall. Though an army encamp against me, my heart shall not fear; though war arise against me, yet I will be confident" (Psalm 27:1-3).

HEBREW WORD HELPS

I will take my stand at my watchpost and *station myself* on the tower, and look out to see what he will say to me, and what I will answer concerning my complaint (Hab. 2:1).

Original Word: צָפָה
Part of Speech: Verb
Transliteration: tsaphah
Phonetic Spelling: (tsaw-faw')
Definition: to look out, spy, keep watch

In this context: *Standing at the ready; attentive*

Whom shall we fear? Indeed! The obvious answer is no one. By the way, the word *stronghold* here comes from the same Hebrew root as *watch post* that we saw in Habakkuk. David had retreated unto his Lord. He was in his sacred place, contemplating all that's happening.

"One thing have I asked of the Lord, that will I seek after: that I may dwell in the house of the Lord all the days of my life, to gaze upon the beauty of the Lord and to inquire in his temple. For he will hide me in his shelter in the day of trouble; he will conceal me under the cover of his tent; he will lift me high upon a rock. And now my head shall be lifted up above my enemies all around me, and I will offer in his tent sacrifices with shouts of joy; I will sing and make melody to the Lord" (27:4-6).

This is a song of praise! Notice how David rests upon what God will do, and then confesses what he will do in response. He's expressed confidence and praise from a place of real struggle:

"Hear, O Lord, when I cry aloud; be gracious to me and answer me! You have said, 'Seek my face.' My heart says to you, 'Your face, Lord, do I seek.' Hide not your face from me. Turn not your servant away in anger, O you who have been my help. Cast me not off; forsake me not, O God of my salvation! For my father and my mother have forsaken me, but the Lord will take me in" (27:7-10).

That's tough to read, isn't it? It's especially difficult if you've ever been there yourself; many of us have been there, and as I've said, sooner or later all of us will. That honesty sets up David's conclusion:

"Teach me your way, O Lord, and lead me on a level path because of my enemies. Give me not up to the will of my adversaries; for false witnesses have risen against me, and they breathe out violence. I believe that I shall look upon the goodness of the Lord in the land of the living! Wait for the Lord; be strong, and let your heart take courage; wait for the Lord!" (27:11-14)

There's an awful lot going on during this season of waiting. The circumstances, though troubling and painful, are bringing forth fruit. In this Psalm's last verse, its crescendo, we read *wait* not once, but twice! And notice there are four verbs in a row in that crescendo: *wait, be strong, take courage, wait.*

That sounds like the words a father would speak to his child: "Wait, be strong, take courage, wait." Parents can offer wise advice because they know more than their children. They understand the bigger picture. "Wait. The end result will be better than what you're experiencing now. Hang in there."

It's not passive waiting that is described there. It's purposeful waiting. It's expectant waiting. That's exactly what we see in Habakkuk, too. "I will station myself on the tower and look out to see." The Hebrew word translated "station myself" is a military term — *standing fast, at the ready.* Then "look out to see" means to *watch intently.* The idea is like leaning forward in eager anticipation — knowing something is going to happen.

A few years ago on opening day of hunting season, my son, Jack, informed me that he wanted to man the tree stand. I told him, "It's not easy — you'll have to be very, very still, and you can't talk." Jack is a lot like his father; he likes to talk. I wasn't sure how he would do. But he did a marvelous job. For several hours, he was absolutely on point! He was purposefully waiting, expectantly waiting, leaning in so as to be sure to see if anything happened. That's the picture Habakkuk gives us.

Habakkuk has retreated to a sacred place, just like David in Psalm 27. Here is another "R" word for you — he begins to *remind* himself just who it is he's waiting on.

Do you remember Habakkuk's approach back in chapter 1? God had just told him what was to unfold. What did the prophet do? He reminded himself of the character traits, the attributes, of God.

"Are you not from everlasting?" He started with the fact that God is the God of all eternity — which certainly includes this moment, the moment of Habakkuk's experiences. Don't forget the context. God had just told him the Babylonians were coming; dreaded and fearsome. Their horses swift, their tactics brutal.

Habakkuk cried out, "O LORD *my* God, *my* Holy One." He reminded himself that God isn't some indifferent and far-removed deity; rather He is a personal and relational God. The prophet declared, "We shall not die," remembering that God is a covenant-keeping God; He hadn't abandoned or forsaken His people.

He reminded himself of God's holiness — "my Holy One." If God is holy, He is also just. He acts justly. That's important to remember, especially in those moments when we don't understand. His holiness is not diminished.

The prophet Isaiah got a glimpse into the throne room of God. He described the scene: the Lord was sitting on the throne; the train of His robe filled the temple. Cherubim surrounded the throne, and they never stopped crying out:

"Holy, holy, holy is the Lord of hosts; the whole earth is full of his glory!" (Isaiah 6:3)

Holy — three times! Repetition like that is a way, in Hebrew, of emphasizing something of great importance and prominence for readers. The apostle John was also given a vision of that scene. He described everything in heaven as oriented toward the One seated on the throne, and a never-ending refrain:

"Holy, holy, holy, is the Lord God Almighty, who was and is and is to come!" (Revelation 4:8)

Consider this: You don't see "love, love, love" or "mercy, mercy, mercy" or "justice, justice, justice" in the Bible. But rather *holiness* — it's an important distinction and reminder. When we can't imagine that God could have allowed this, we need to remind ourselves that He's absolutely holy.

Right after declaring God is "my Holy One," Habakkuk reminds himself, "O Lord, you have ordained [these events]." The word *ordained* means fixed, appointed, put in place.

God is holy, and God is sovereign. So let this sink in: He has appointed this; He has allowed it to happen. You have to allow your mind to go there.

By reminding himself that God is everlasting, holy, and sovereign, Habakkuk begins to understand much deeper truth: the Babylonians have been established not by chance or by might, but by the hand of God. The calamity they've brought against Judah is by God's design.

As Habakkuk wraps his mind around this, he's — a third "R" word — *rethinking* things. He retreats, reminds, then rethinks.

It is important to grasp the concept of rethinking because of what happens when things go off the tracks. When we find ourselves overwhelmed, we tend to lose sight of the character and attributes of our God, His faithfulness and omnipotence. The problems consume us; the issues crush us. The next thing we know, those things develop into worry and anxiety. We're tempted to take things into our own hands, all the while becoming more frustrated than ever before.

Rethinking is the path to acknowledging that God's plans are much greater than our own. God's plan was to use the Babylonians as a tool. Habakkuk knew that it was going to happen, but he didn't understand why.

But he trusted God. How do we know that? Notice the "I will" statements: "*I will* take my stand at the watch post." It's implied for each phrase: "*I will* station myself on the tower. *I will* look out to see what he will say, and *I will* answer." This is a statement of action, of trust.

What Do You Know?

Habakkuk's thought process and response are unfolding before our eyes. As he's rethinking, his understanding of God is broadening, and that produces a newer outworking of all of this in his life. When you have the wrong idea — or an uninformed idea — of God, it leads to a wrong outworking. When you find yourself asking these desperate *Why?* questions, and when they lead you to deeper moral questions of God, a wrong understanding of God can spin you out of control.

We must always come back to the reality of who our God is. We see Habakkuk do just that, and then — this verse ends with one last "R" — he *recommits* himself as a follower of God. He retreats, reminds, rethinks, recommits.

Over and again, Habakkuk said, "I will." Each of these phrases appears in the imperfect tense. In the English language, we're familiar with three tenses: past, present, and future. They all have to do with time. In Hebrew they have two, perfect and imperfect. Perfect and imperfect don't have as much to do with time as they do with action. Perfect tense speaks of completeness, or action concluded. The imperfect tense communicates incompleteness, or action still ongoing.

When you look at this text through the lens of a little bit of grammatical knowledge, you come away with a panoramic view of what's happening in Habakkuk. The imperfect tense speaks of continuation. It's like saying, "I will take my stand, and I will continue to take my stand." With each "I will" in this verse, Habakkuk is stressing continuation. You're the Holy God — *I will wait* — *and continue to wait* — for your answer.

The essence, then, of what he says — and what you and I need to hear — at the end of this verse is: "Once I have come to this point, once I have stationed myself, once I have looked out, I am ready for, waiting for, actively pursuing the response of God, then I'm willing to see how I'll answer!" He's recommitting. He is bolstering himself up in the knowledge of his God.

Recommitment is something that occurs over and over and over again in the Christian life. Do you remember when you first met the Lord? Do you remember the commitment that you gave to Him? How excited, passionate, and on fire you were? Not long after that, you experienced the pull of the world. You found yourself stumbling again into unfaithfulness and unrighteousness. What do you do? You repent; you go back and recommit yourself to God.

It's life: commitment and recommitment, commitment and recommitment. If you're married, you committed yourself to that man or that woman. In short order, you found out they're just as flawed as you are. You had to recommit yourself. Don't feel bad. Your spouse has had to recommit too! You recommit yourself to parenting. When your son or daughter hits the "Terrible Twos," you recommit to parenting out of faith and not fear. When they hit their teens? Recommit, recommit, recommit! You recommit to a healthy diet. You recommit to exercise. You recommit to savings.

When times are the absolute toughest, we retreat, remind ourselves, rethink things, and recommit: "God, you're the One who holds the everlasting future!"

This is life. This is the Christian life. At some point or another, we all find ourselves here. Maybe you're at that very point right now. Maybe you're praying for a friend or loved one who stands at the brink. Now you know where to go when things go desperately wrong.

Once you're retreated, you're reminded, you're rethinking, the next step is intuitive — time to recommit. You know it. And not a moment too soon! Beginning with the very next verse, Habakkuk hears God's specific answer.

3

Two Paths

Habakkuk opened, you'll recall, with a great cry of pathos, this deeply emotional question, "Why?" The prophet asked the Lord, "How long must I cry for help? Why do you make me see iniquity? Why do you make me look at the wrong?" And he asked over and over again.

Judah was going through a painful transition. King Josiah — the righteous king — was killed in battle. He had been leading the country back toward God, but now Habakkuk watched as the country was falling hard in every way possible, especially in a spiritual sense. He saw the dreaded Babylonians were sweeping forward and that Judah was next in their path. Habakkuk cried out "Why?" and he received an answer — but not the answer he expected.

God said, "Behold, I am the one raising up the Chaldeans." In other words, "I am behind the evil oppressor that is going to sweep through and take Judah away." Habakkuk was dumbfounded. God's answer gave rise to even more questions — those of a moral nature: "Why God? How could you? Are you righteous? Are you fair? Are you just?"

It's the moral questions that make Habakkuk such a modern and relevant book. These are the questions we ask: "Why, God, do you allow crises into our lives? How do I understand you as a good God in the midst of all this?"

Moral questions like that move us to a place of waiting, as we saw with the prophet. He determined to station himself — to actively watch and wait — for God's answer. God's specific answer to Habakkuk becomes a turning point in the book, and yields a turning point for us as Christ-followers when we're left wondering, "What do we do in the face of calamity?" or "What do we do in times of uncertainty?"

Write This Down

Through the first chapter of Habakkuk, God hadn't answered the prophet specifically. He had, however, laid a sure foundation: I am in control. I have a divine plan. I have a divine reason. I have a divine timetable. The prophet expected God's specific answer would come, and so he prepared himself — you remember the four 'R' words we discovered in Habakkuk's anticipation: retreat, remind, rethink, recommit.

Habakkuk tells us what happened next:

"And the Lord answered me: 'Write the vision; make it plain on tablets, so he may run who reads it. For still the vision awaits its appointed time; it hastens to the end — it will not lie. If it seems slow, wait for it; it will surely come; it will not delay'" (Habakkuk 2:2-3).

There's that sense of waiting, wrapped up in the foundational truths: God is in control and has a divine plan, divine reason, and a divine timetable. There is an assurance that everything is moving forward. And there is an admonition that we should not count God as slow as some count slowness.

Peter, in his writings, echoed that counsel, and gave a compelling context in which to view waiting on the Lord:

"But do not overlook this one fact, beloved, that with the Lord one day is as a thousand years, and a thousand years as one day. The Lord is not slow to fulfill his promise as some count slowness, but is patient toward you, not wishing that any should perish, but that all should reach repentance" (2 Peter 3:8-9).

Behind it all, there is a redemptive bigger picture. He is a God who will keep his promises. We need to remember that in our lives. We need to remember that in the whole scheme of life. God has promised to keep us; he will keep us. He promised to send His Son to return; He will send His Son to return. It may seem slow to us, but God is faithful. It's there in the text. That's exactly what he said to Habakkuk. He continues:

"Behold, his soul is puffed up; it is not upright within him, but the righteous shall live by his faith. Moreover, wine is a traitor, an arrogant man who is never at rest. His greed is as wide as Sheol; like death he has never enough. He gathers for himself all nations and collects as his own all peoples" (2:4-5).

At this point, we need to pay close attention to the pronouns or we may get confused. What is God saying? Who is He talking about? He is presenting a contrast — juxtaposing two ways: the way of the Babylonians versus the way of the righteous.

"His soul is puffed up." Whose soul? The Babylonians' soul. You remember, Babylon was catching up all the peoples in their path, with revelry and rejoicing, praising their war machine. Puffed up! Before moving on, let's linger for a moment on this image of the Babylonians bloated with pride.

The Hebrew language is very poetic. It creates pictures. The word rendered "puffed up," for instance, means bloated up — like a dead animal bloats up on the side of the road. Perhaps a small animal hit by a car, its stomach distended, swollen. You know what's happening there — maggots are in there eating away. I've probably just ruined your appetite, but the point is, it's a graphic picture: Babylon is so puffed up with pride, they're ready to burst.

The Babylonian soul is crooked within him. It's not straight. It's not trustworthy. It's puffed up with pride — and it's imbibed with wine. Did you notice the phrase, "moreover, wine is a traitor"? There is a passage in the book of Daniel that gives us an idea of what God was conveying:

"King Belshazzar made a great feast for a thousand of his lords and drank wine in front of the thousand. Belshazzar, when he tasted the wine, commanded that the vessels of gold and of silver that Nebuchadnezzar his father had taken out of the temple in Jerusalem be brought, that the king and his lords, his wives, and his concubines might drink from them. Then they brought in the golden vessels that had been taken out of the temple, the house of God in Jerusalem, and the king and his lords, his wives, and his concubines drank from them. They drank wine and praised the gods of gold and silver, bronze, iron, wood, and stone" (Daniel 5:1-4).

That scene from Daniel of Belshazzar's wine feast is consistent with the picture historians have painted of Babylonian culture, steeped in drunkenness and debauchery.

The description is that of "an arrogant man" who is "greedy" and "never has enough." God puts into words what Habakkuk and others in that day had seen — Babylon was devouring every nation and people in their way. The Babylonians were a war machine, and they were bearing down on Judah to take them into captivity. That's one part of the contrast — one way.

And please don't miss the word "but" that God used to introduce the juxtaposition. Here's a graphic description of Babylonian way, "but the righteous shall live by his faith." There's the other way. There's the contrast.

God said in essence, "Habakkuk, do you see the Babylonians? That is not the path of life. There is another path — it's the path of my chosen ones. It's the way of faith. The righteous shall live by faith." And that, my friends, is how we are to live when facing calamity or enduring seasons of uncertainty.

I cannot overstate the importance of the phrase "the righteous shall live by faith." There are some scholars who believe it is the most important phrase in the entire Bible. Imagine that! We can say this with confidence: It's important enough that it was repeated three times in the New Testament.

A Reformation

What does it mean? "The righteous shall live by faith" speaks of the very beginning of our relationship with God — we come to God through faith. But it also speaks of the continuation of that relationship — we walk with God in faith. It is instruction for how we should live. It's the very core of the Christian life. It was at the very core of an issue that transformed a man named Martin Luther, and through him, the Church.

Most people think of October 31 as Halloween — or All Hallows Eve, the evening before All Saints Day. In the history of the Church, October 31 is known as Reformation Day. It was on that day in 1517 that Martin Luther nailed *The 95 Theses* on the door of the church at Wittenberg. A little backstory is in order.

A year earlier, in 1516, a friar by the name of Johann Tetzel was sent to Germany to raise money to rebuild St. Peter's Basilica in Rome. He was officially a "papal commissioner for indulgences." The Church said the purchase of indulgences would move God in forgiving sins — yours or those of loved ones who had passed away, thus releasing them from a purgatory state. A popular saying attributed to Tetzel went, "As soon as the coin in the coffer rings, the soul from purgatory springs."

In response, Luther wrote a letter entitled "Disputation of Martin Luther on the Power and Efficacy of Indulgences," which became popularly known as *The 95 Theses*. Make no mistake, the letter was a strong protest. Thesis 86, for example, asked: "Why does the pope, whose wealth today is greater than the wealth of the richest Crassus, build the basilica of St. Peter with the money of poor believers rather than with his own money?"

The Catholic Church was teaching faith + works. Luther stood against the tide. He said, "It's faith + nothing!" Faith alone! *Sola fide!*

Luther's protest took flight — it became one of the first controversies in history aided by the printing press. Within mere days, copies of *The 95 Theses* were distributed throughout Germany, and in a matter of weeks, across Europe.

Martin Luther is called the Father of the Protestant Reformation. And we're protestors still today! What are we protesting? We protest anything different than what God teaches in the phrase, "the righteous shall live by faith."

Imagine the conviction it took to stand in the face of everyone else — kings, rulers, magistrates, and the Pope himself — and say, "I'm right on this and you're all wrong!"

It will be helpful to understand how Martin Luther arrived there; to be so determined that it was his way, and no one else's.

Martin's father, Hans, was a coal miner. That would make Martin's sister … a coal miner's daughter!

Hans was a hard-working miner desiring a better life for his son. He put in long hours and saved money so he could send young Martin away to Law School. Martin excelled as a lawyer, even beyond his peers. He gained a firm grasp of the law in his mind, and that would transform the way he understood God.

Luther lived during a highly superstitious age. Even those who belonged to the Church and followed Christ believed all kinds of strange things. There was widespread confusion about God's judgment, and specifically how He dealt with His children.

We catch a glimpse of this from Luther's "calling to ministry." As a young man in his early 20s, Martin was returning from a visit to his parents' home when a violent thunderstorm erupted. He believed the storm was God, bringing vengeance upon him. He wrote in his journal that bolts of lightning struck right beside him. In great fear, he hid beneath a tree and cried out to God through St. Anne, the patron saint of miners. "St. Anne, may God help me? I will become a monk!" He was desperate, and so he made a radical promise.

Have you ever been in a situation in which you've made a radical promise to God? "God, if you'll just get me out of this, I'll serve you!" Have you ever done that before? Usually, when we come to our senses, we rationalize that it was just a moment in time, and we liberate ourselves from the obligation. Not Martin Luther.

Luther went home that day and began to give away his things. He traveled to the law school, picked up his books — which his father had paid for — and gifted them to his classmates. He gave away his clothing. He rid himself of almost all his material possessions, and, two weeks later, he entered an Augustinian monastery. He presented himself before the church to serve as a monk — a man of his word.

Recognize, though, that he became a monk so that he would earn his way into heaven. He did this so he could earn, in a sense, righteous standing before the angry God he had perceived in his mind. His own writings reveal that "I kept the rule of my order so strictly that if ever a monk got to heaven by monkery, it was I."

The stories about Luther at the monastery are legendary and further reveal the process he went through.

In his writings, Martin Luther described his time at the confessional. Every morning, the monks were required to go before the priests and to confess their sins. What kind of trouble do you suppose you can you get into at a monastery? Perhaps, "I coveted brother Andrew's soup last night," or "I like brother Phillip's robe better than my own." How much can monks have to confess? It must have gone quick: they'd duck in, confess, and be off to work.

Not Luther! He went into those confessionals — he didn't just stay there for five minutes, or 10 minutes, or 30 — he'd stay there for an hour, an hour and a half, two hours, three! It drove his superiors crazy! They had to wonder, "Why are you so concerned with these bitty little sins?"

Luther's times of confession were considered "marathon confessions." But remember, Luther possessed a sharp, legal mind. He considered what he had done before the righteousness of God, and was compelled to confess each and every small detail. Why? So that he might earn a sense of righteousness before God. This was Luther! He took that sharply trained mind and applied it to the law of God — the law that demands perfection — and realized he didn't measure up.

Another story recalls his first mass as he transitioned from monk to priest. In the Catholic tradition, what happens during the mass is known as transubstantiation — they believe that the body and blood of Christ take on the corporeal nature of the elements, bread and wine. In other words, at first it looks like bread and wine, but then when the priests offer the words of consecration, they became the Lord's body and blood.

The priest would raise the bread and speak in Latin, "Hoc est corpus meum," which means, "This is my body." In that instant, the elements no longer just signified but actually became Christ. (A bit of an aside for you: it has been suggested the words "Hocus Pocus" spoken by magicians in magic shows were originally a parody of the priest's consecration in Latin — the simile to suggest, "Something amazing or even miraculous is taking place at this moment, right before your very eyes.")

As he was preparing to administer his first mass, Luther became overwhelmed with doubt: "How could a sinful man like me hold the body and blood of Christ?" When he picked up the cup, convinced that this was the blood of Jesus Christ, he began to shake. He shook so badly, the cup began to spill.

It was a devastating experience. Luther's superior recognized the difficulty he was having. He recognized also his new priest's giftedness. He sent Luther to the university to study theology. It turned out to be the best thing — it was at the university that Martin Luther first held a Bible in his hands.

Reading that Bible, it was when Martin Luther got to Habakkuk 2:4 — "the righteous shall live by faith" — that he realized: it's not about a righteousness we create before God, but rather it's a righteousness God gives.

A short time later, Luther's superiors sent him to Rome. While crossing the Alps he became violently ill — he believed he was going to die. He said of that experience, the only thing that gave him comfort was those words: "the righteous shall live by faith."

One more experience cemented Luther's theological awakening. While in Rome, he visited the Scala Sancta at St. John's Lateran Church. The Scala Sancta is a set of stairs that, according to Catholic tradition, are the steps that led up to the praetorium of Pontius Pilate in Jerusalem, those which Jesus climbed making His way to trial. Since those steps were moved to Rome in the Fourth Century, devout Catholics have made a pilgrimage to see them.

To this day, you can visit Scala Sancta, and you'll see many devotees crawling up those stairs on their hands and knees. They pause at certain points where there are little panes of glass, said to cover spots where drops of Jesus' blood had fallen. You'll see the people stop, bend, and kiss those panes of glass. Why do they do it? The Church granted indulgences to pilgrims who climbed the stairs on their knees.

So there was Martin Luther, at Scala Sancta. He was making his way up the stairs, stopping, bending, and kissing — just like everyone else. He noticed the peasants who had made the pilgrimage, and who had spent money — money they didn't have — to purchase indulgences.

When he was just about to the top of the steps, he stood up and took that indulgence, that simple piece of paper he had purchased from the church steps below, wadded it up in his hands and dropped it down. As Martin Luther looked back over the steps, and at all the pilgrims who were climbing on their knees, he saw the reality of Habakkuk 2:4 — the righteous shall not live by the acts of righteousness that they do, "but the righteous shall live by faith."

He wrote of that experience: "At that moment it broke into my mind and I realized for the first time that my justification and my station before God is established not on the basis of my own naked righteousness, which will always fall short of the commands of God, but that it rests solely on the righteousness of Christ which I must hold onto by trusting in faith. And when I understood that," he wrote, "I understood the gospel and I looked and beheld the doors of paradise were swinging open to me and I walked through."

That's why it's called a reformation. It's not by our works, but by faith. And it's a faith that's not even our own — it is given to us by God. When Luther nailed *The 95 Theses* on the door at Wittenberg, he was saying the Church, which was supposed to be the purveyor or carrier of faith, had misled the people. He decided to stand against it. The gospel — the gospel of *sola fide* — sets men free!

Tell Us What You Really Think

The Catholic Church didn't take Luther's actions lightly. Pope Leo X declared that Luther was "a wild boar, loose in the kingdom of God." The pope excommunicated him, which meant he was under the threat of being burned at the stake. Luther engaged in many dialogues and debates seeking resolution, all the while the tension escalated. Finally he was summoned to appear at the Diet of Worms — a formal, deliberative assembly — to either recant or reaffirm his views. Luther knew that his refusal to recant could well cost him his life.

In anticipation of his appearance, the groundswell of reformation was rising. The people were with him. Many asked, "Luther, what are you going to say when you get to Worms?" Committed deeply to his theology, he replied, "I used to speak of the pope as the Vicar of Christ, but now I'm going to say that the pope is the adversary of Christ, the Vicar of Satan." Those sound like fighting words, don't they?

At this point, Hollywood scripts would have you believe that Luther marched in, stood before the magistrates, princes, the king, and all those who represented the Church. They very dramatically demanded, "Martin Luther, will you recant of these writings?" to which he, even more dramatically replied, "Unless I'm convinced of sacred Scripture by evident reason, I will not recant." Boom! The Reformation was born!

But that's now how it went down. In reality, it was quite different.

They did bring him before the assembly and demand, "Martin Luther, will you recant?" But do you know what he said in response? They didn't know — he spoke so softly they had to ask him to repeat himself. He spoke softly again. Finally they said, "Speak up! Will you recant?" Martin Luther's answer — the answer that launched the Reformation — was, "May I have 24 hours to think about it?"

Luther went back to his cell to pray and meditate over his answer. That night he wrote out a prayer that survives to this day. He prayed:

O God, Almighty! God everlasting! How dreadful is the world! Behold how its mouth opens to swallow me up, and how small is my faith in Thee! O the weakness of the flesh, and the power of Satan! If I am to depend upon any strength of this world — all is over. O God! O God! O thou, my God help me against the wisdom of this world. Do this I beseech Thee. The work is not mine, but Thine. I have no business here. I have nothing to contend for with these great men of the world. I would gladly pass my days in happiness and peace. But the cause is Thine. And it is righteous and everlasting! O Lord help me! O faithful and unchangeable God I lean not upon man. My God, my God, dost Thou not hear me? My God art Thou no longer living? The complaint of the prophet goes and says, "Thou hast chosen me for this work. I know it, therefore O God accomplish Thine own will. Forsake me not, for the sake of thy well-beloved Son, Jesus Christ, my defense, my buckler, and my stronghold. Lord – where are thou?"

Did you notice that Luther's prayer sounds a lot like Habakkuk?

"Dost Thou not hear me? Art Thou no longer living?" Hello?!?

The next day Luther returned to the hall at the Diet of Worms. The inquisitor put forth the question, "Will you recant?" Martin Luther hesitated for a moment, then answered: "Unless I am convinced of Sacred Scripture or by evident reason, I cannot recant. For my conscience is held captive by the Word of God and to act against conscience is neither right nor safe. Here I stand. I can do no other. God help me."

In a moment of crisis, what do you do? Habakkuk 2:4 says, "the righteous shall live by his faith." Let the weight of that sink in. We not only come to God through faith, but we also live out our lives in faith. And to be absolutely clear: faith + nothing! *Sola fide!*

And many of us have been there: Your relationship is over. You're on the brink. Your child is dying and you can't stop it. You're at the brink. Your job, your income, your future is ripped out from under you. You're at the brink. You leave the doctors' office with the diagnosis. You're at the brink. Any number of scenarios, as many and varied as souls reading these words — what do we do at the brink?

We go back to this truth: the righteous — that's you — live by faith. You live your life by the very same faith that you have in Him for your salvation. You walk by faith.

4

Path One

We considered how Habakkuk 2:4 impacted Martin Luther. The truth in that verse changed the trajectory of his theology, which directly impacts our theology today as Protestants.

Let's come back to the sense of the text in its context. When I read, "the righteous shall live by his faith," I immediately begin to ask a number of questions. Who are the righteous? What is faith? How do I live by my faith? These are important questions. They're questions that we need to answer if we're going to fully understand the ramifications of the passage itself.

Let me tell you how important this is: if you understand this truth, you understand the Gospel of the Lord Jesus Christ. You understand the Gospel as it was revealed in the Old Covenant and the Old Testament, and as it unfolds in the New Covenant and the New Testament — fulfilled in Jesus Christ! We need to ask the questions,

"What does this mean?" and "How do I apply it in my life?"

I mentioned already that the phrase "the righteous shall live by faith" is repeated three times in the New Testament. You'll find it in Romans 1:17, Galatians 3:11, and Hebrews 10:38. That's important to note because when you study scripture, it is its own best commentary.

So if you read Habakkuk 2:4 and come away with questions like "Who are the righteous?" and "What does it mean to live by faith?" you can expect that other scripture passages will help you answer those questions. A great place to start is in those three texts where the verse is repeated.

Forensic Righteousness

That first question, "Who are the righteous?" That question bothered Martin Luther. He doubted that he could attain God's standard of righteousness. He knew he was never going to be good enough. You saw that clearly in his marathon confessions and in the inner conflict that raged as he regarded the body and blood of Christ during his mass.

How can a sinner obtain righteousness from a God who demands sinless perfection? That was Luther's dilemma. It's a vitally important question, but one very few people are asking today. Do you know why? Most people don't believe there is a righteousness issue because they don't believe there is a sin issue.

Ligonier Ministries — R.C. Sproul's organization — put out a report on this subject. They did a study in which they asked: "Is the smallest sin deserving of hell?" Only 18% of those who responded said "Yes." Another number in that report is even more telling: only 51% of people who identified themselves as Protestant Evangelicals answered "Yes" to the question, "Is the smallest sin deserving of hell?" If you read your Bible, you know better.

In that same study people were asked: "Everyone sins a little, but do you believe that in that littleness, they are basically good?" 67% agreed — man is basically good. 44% of Protestant Evangelicals answered that man is good. This is a problem. That's not what the Scriptures teach us.

Consider these words from King David concerning the origin of our sin:

"Behold, I was brought forth in iniquity, and in sin did my mother conceive me" (Psalm 51:5).

You weren't born good. You weren't even born neutral. You were born into sin. The theological term for that is depravity. Because of Adam's sin, it's been passed on to you. It's not waiting for a moment in time when you commit a sin — you were born into sin, conceived in sin, actually. You may have been an adorable little baby, but you were born in sin, nonetheless.

In the apostle Paul's letter to the church at Rome, the theme of chapter 3 is God's righteousness, and a major premise is that none of us are born righteous. Speaking of humanity, he says:

"As it is written: 'None are righteous, no, not one; no one understands; no one seeks for God. All have turned aside; together they have become worthless; no one does good, not even one'" (Romans 3:10-12).

You could continue reading, and the next several verses only add weight — we are not righteous, we're not able to be righteous, and we are not good in God's eyes. Now that doesn't mean we can't do good things. It means that in light of the standard of God's righteousness, when it comes to salvation, we are, as Paul said in his letter to the church at Ephesus, "dead in our trespasses" (Ephesians 2:5). Depravity!

Why is this important? Why do we look at these passages and cross-reference them? Because we live in an age where theology is no longer learned from scripture, but from culture. Culture says we human beings are basically good. The Bible tells us we're not. The Bible tells us that we are left wanting before God. Habakkuk understood that.

When God spoke into Habakkuk's situation, He was not only speaking into the national crisis, but also into the sin crisis. Habakkuk had to wonder, "If you are a righteous God, how can I — a sinful man — have a relationship with you?" That's a great question for us to ask. It's a question that the Bible definitively answers.

Let's look at the first of those three passages where the phrase from Habakkuk 2:4 is repeated — in the first chapter of Paul's letter to the church at Rome. He said:

"For I am not ashamed of the gospel, for it is the power of God for salvation to everyone who believes, to the Jew first and also to the Greek. For in it the righteousness of God is revealed from faith for faith, as it is written, 'The righteous shall live by faith'" (Romans 1:16-17).

Paul wasn't ashamed of the Gospel. He recognized there is power in it — it leads to salvation! Paul is also saying that this is the *only*

Gospel — it's the only power that leads to salvation. It's not one of many. There is no other. In it, the righteousness of God is revealed. There's good news! And it's revealed from faith to faith, just as it is written — guess where? He echoes the words of God spoken to Habakkuk.

What does Paul mean when he speaks of righteousness? The Greek word translated "righteous" here, according to a Greek/English Lexicon, means "to cause someone to be in a proper or right relationship with another; a forensic righteousness."

That's a very curious term: *a forensic righteousness*. That sounds sort of like something you might see on the television show *CSI*. If you're not familiar with the show, it's about a forensic team that uses scientific processes to gather information and evidence to prosecute

GREEK WORD HELPS

For in it the *righteousness* of God is revealed from faith for faith, as it is written, "The righteous shall live by faith." (Rom. 1:17)

Original Word: δικαιοσύνη, ης, ἡ
Part of Speech: Noun, Fem.
Transliteration: dikaiosuné
Phonetic Spelling: (dik-ah-yos-oo′-nay)
Definition: justness, righteousness of which God is the source or author, but practically: a divine righteousness.

In this context: *determined just by God; justness originated in God*

WHEN YOUR CIRCUMSTANCES CHALLENGE THE PROMISES OF GOD

crimes. A judge, then, looks at the evidence and renders a verdict.

When the word *forensic* is applied to our righteousness, it suggests that the pathology is clear: this is a God thing. You'd recognize in your state of sin that the judge should easily and swiftly declare you guilty and bring punishment down on you. He has every right to do it.

But Paul says that this is a forensic righteousness. You've been declared not guilty! Years ago, during the O.J. Simpson murder trial, famed defense attorney Johnny Cochrane made the famous "If it don't fit, you must acquit!" closing argument. Apply it here: your definition of your life as "unrighteous" doesn't fit anymore. You are a Christ-follower. A new definition has been applied to you: you're now "a righteous one."

Still doubt it? Look back to Romans 3. Paul made the case: no one is righteous, no not one. Verse after verse of stinging indictment, concluding:

> "Now we know that whatever the law says it speaks to those who are under the law, so that every mouth may be stopped, and the whole world may be held accountable to God. For by works of the law no human being will be justified in his sight, since through the law comes knowledge of sin" (Romans 3:19-20).

No human being will be justified. We are hopelessly lost in and of ourselves. This would be a wonderful place for a conjunction, wouldn't it?

> "But now the righteousness of God has been manifested apart from the law, although the Law and the Prophets bear

witness to it — the righteousness of God through faith in Jesus Christ for all who believe" (Romans 3:21-22).

Here's the working of Christ in your life. You've been made righteous. Listen, by the imputation of Christ — another theological term — Christ has transferred His righteousness on to you! By faith! Which, by the way, is also a gift of God, not something that we, in and of ourselves, have attained.

As part of this miraculous transaction, God also transferred our unrighteousness onto Christ, who paid for it at the cross. If you are a follower of Jesus Christ, you are a follower by faith. In that faith, an imputation — or a transfer — has taken place. Peter explained it like this:

"He himself bore our sins in his body on the tree, that we might die to sin and live to righteousness. By his wounds you have been healed" (1 Peter 2:24).

Paul summed it up this way:

"But the free gift is not like the trespass. For if many died through one man's trespass, much more have the grace of God and the free gift by the grace of that one man Jesus Christ abounded for many" (Romans 5:15).

How do you relate to God? In Christ! How does God relate to you? Through Christ! He now sees you as righteous. A justified person no longer tries to please God to gain salvation on his or her own merit, but rather by faith clings to Christ. That's what it means to be one who is righteous. It's not a righteousness of your own. It's a righteousness applied to you. It's the righteousness of Christ! That is the Gospel!

If anyone tells you that you must do certain deeds; you must cut out certain activities; you must perform in certain ways to receive the righteousness of God in your life — they speak another gospel. That's an anathema — it's a damnable gospel! The one true Gospel says that it is by faith and by faith alone in Jesus Christ that you are made righteous!

Faith

What is faith? That's the question we should be asking next. To answer that question, we can turn to the book of Hebrews.

You'll remember that we discovered chapter-and-verse divisions in our Bibles weren't part of the original. Editors added them to help us navigate and locate passages. Every now and then they seem to break up a thought in a way that the writer might not have intended. We'll see another of those, here.

> "For, 'Yet a little while, and the coming one will come and will not delay; but my righteous one shall live by faith, and if he shrinks back, my soul has no pleasure in him.' But we are not of those who shrink back and are destroyed, but of those who have faith and preserve their souls. Now faith is the assurance of things hoped for, the conviction of things not seen" (Hebrews 10:37-11:1).

You see the Habakkuk 2:4 mention. Here's a great example of

scripture being its own best commentary. What is the definition of faith? That last verse — the assurance of things hoped for and the conviction of things not seen.

I like Dr. James Boyce's definition of faith. He takes all of Hebrews 10:37 through Hebrews 11:1, and he pulls it together into one definition: "faith is believing God and acting upon that belief." We do not shrink back, but we live by that faith. Do you want to see examples of that faith being lived out? The writer of Hebrews gave them to us over and over with the remainder of chapter 11.

Hebrews 11 is often called the "Hall of Faith," as in it one example after another is given of men and women who expressed their faith in their actions. Perhaps you've never thought about it in this way: Each of them is commended for what they did. Each did something that articulated the authenticity of their faith.

Abel is mentioned. What did he do? He offered God a more suitable sacrifice than his brother Cain. Abel believed God and acted on it. There was an authenticity to his faith: he lived it out.

Noah is mentioned. God warned Noah concerning events yet unseen. In reverent fear, Noah constructed an ark, and saved the members of his household. He believed God. He authenticated it by what he did.

Abraham is in the Hall of Faith. He obeyed God when he was called out — to a place unseen, by the way — where he was to receive an inheritance. Abraham believed God and demonstrated it to be true through his obedience. In so many steps along the way in Abraham's journey, his faith was seen: he moved to a promised land because God told him to; he lived there as a foreigner; he trusted God in the conception of his son Isaac; he trusted God, willing to sacrifice his son. These were all telling articulations of his faith — it wasn't just something he gave ascent to mentally; it was something he lived out.

The Hall of Faith goes on: Isaac believed God and blessed Jacob and Esau. Moses believed God and left Egypt. Please don't miss this: faith is always associated with action. It's never about giving a simple intellectual ascent. The Reformers were fond of saying, "It is faith alone, but it is not a faith that is alone." In other words, you come to Christ by faith alone, but if it's a true faith, it will demonstrate itself. It will be lived out.

If we have asked the questions "Who are the righteous?" and "What is faith?" then the next logical question becomes, "How do I live by that faith?" A third reference to Habakkuk 2:4, this one found in Paul's letter to the church at Galatia, will shed some light. First, a little backstory on the book of Galatians will be helpful.

The book of Galatians stresses one principle over and over: live out your faith! Paul had been to Galatia during his early missionary travels. He taught them salvation by faith alone. He taught them Jesus' resurrection. He taught them about the new life. He taught them about the Holy Spirit. He taught them about Christ's return.

Somewhere after his departure, the church in Galatia started to fall back into many of the Jewish ordinances and practices — rules that said it was necessary to do certain things to earn God's favor. When Paul learned of this he was outraged. Take a look:

"O foolish Galatians! Who has bewitched you? It was before your eyes that Jesus Christ was publicly portrayed as crucified. Let me ask you only this: Did you receive the Spirit by works of the law or by hearing with faith? Are you so foolish? Having begun by the Spirit, are you now being perfected by the flesh?" (Galatians 3:1-3)

Please don't miss what Paul is saying. We begin by faith — it's by faith alone that you are saved. And it's by faith that you live. You don't go forward trying, now, to perfect your faith in the flesh — by the stuff you do. So here, now, is the third echo of Habakkuk 2:4:

> "For all who rely on works of the law are under a curse; for it is written, 'Cursed be everyone who does not abide by all things written in the Book of the Law, and do them.' Now it is evident that no one is justified before God by the law, for 'The righteous shall live by faith'" (Galatians 3:10-11).

To reiterate the point — by faith and faith alone — Paul stressed:

> "For freedom Christ has set us free; stand firm therefore and do not submit again to a yoke of slavery" (Galatians 5:1).

He minced no words concerning those who attempted to clutter up the Gospel message — those who attempted to make it a matter of faith + anything else. Tell us how you really feel, Paul! Near the close of his letter he addressed those in Galatia who were teaching that new believers must submit to circumcision in order to be squarely in God's favor:

> "I wish those who unsettle you would emasculate themselves!" (Galatians 5:12)

Again and again: don't be misled into the idea that you must do certain acts of righteousness to be saved or to earn God's favor. But please be clear, while Paul preached salvation is by faith alone, it was not a faith that is alone. He clarified:

> "Walk by the Spirit that you will not gratify the desires of the flesh" (Galatians 5:16).

The apostle Paul expected that a person of faith would live out their faith strategically acting in righteousness. In other words, it's not work that saves you, but it demonstrates that you're saved. So here's the question: Are you a person of faith? If you answer "Yes!" then I'd say, "Amen!"

Take An Inventory

Do you then live out that faith? Here is where that old preacher adage comes in: "Well now you're stepping on my toes!" But this is a question we have to ask. Are you clinging to faith that is all in your mind? Or do you see a living, vibrant faith played out in how you live and what you do? Are you living by the Spirit? Walking by the Spirit? Is your desire to walk in righteousness?

That is what God is saying to Habakkuk: my chosen people — the righteous ones who are righteous by faith alone — they're going to live by that faith.

You see, the great call of the Gospel in our lives is to cling to it. Not by works, lest any man should boast. But what does the Scripture say? We should walk in righteousness. So here's a question to ask yourself: "Am I walking in righteousness?" It's faith alone, but not a faith that is alone.

You don't want to come to the end of your life clinging to something that has never borne fruit. You want to come to the end of your life and meet your Heavenly Father, who receives you and says, "Well done, my good and faithful servant. By faith enter into your reward."

5

Path Two

So how do we live? We live by faith. That's where our relationship with God starts. That's how our relationship with God continues. It's by faith. But if you remember, back in chapter 3, we approached Habakkuk 2:4-5 as it appears — as part of a contrast.

God painted a picture for Habakkuk by contrasting two paths: the way Judah should live and the way the Babylonians lived. You could think of it as Judah's belief versus Babylon's non-belief, or the way of faith versus the way of non-faith.

The next passage we encounter moving through Habakkuk 2 is called the "Taunt Song." You'll find passages like this throughout Scripture — songs sung by oppressed people to their captors. What's interesting to note here is that this song is from God to the Babylonians; not written by a prophet or a psalmist, but God Himself is the songwriter. He's calling His people, Judah, to sing along with Him.

A taunt song — particularly this one — is a song of judgment. It announces what will soon take place. In this passage, you'll notice the word "woe" often repeated. You'll see it in verses 6, 9, 12, 15, and 19. It says, "Let there be no doubt: Judgment is coming to you Babylonians! Woe to you!" In this song, God grants Habakkuk — and Judah — a look into the future.

Sing Along

"Shall not all these take up their taunt against him, with scoffing and riddles for him, and say, 'Woe to him who heaps up what is not his own — for how long? — and loads himself with pledges!' Will not your debtors suddenly arise and those awake who will make you tremble? Then you will be spoil for them. Because you have plundered many nations, all the remnant of the peoples shall plunder you, for the blood of man and violence to the earth, to cities and all who dwell in them" (Habakkuk 2:6-8).

Habakkuk had stationed himself and was waiting for God's answer — Why? How? Do you see this injustice, God? Can you possibly turn a blind eye? Those are the sorts of moral questions that must have been surfacing in his mind. God's answer, from the start, assures that He not only sees, but also that Babylon will have to answer for it. With this first woe, God charges the wicked in their all-consuming greed for power and possessions. But He's just getting started.

"Woe to him who gets evil gain for his house, to set his nest on high, to be safe from the reach of harm! You have devised shame for your house by cutting off many peoples; you have forfeited your life. For the stone will cry out from the wall, and the beam from the woodwork respond" (2:9-11).

In the song's second woe, God indicts Babylon for the belief that they'd created an impregnable empire, and for having endeavored to do it at the expense of others. This brings shame, not glory. The picture is made even more graphic by the personification of inanimate objects — the shame will be so thoroughgoing that even the ill-gotten materials themselves, the stones, beams, and woodwork, will join in the taunt song.

"Woe to him who builds a town with blood and founds a city on iniquity! Behold, is it not from the Lord of hosts that peoples labor merely for fire, and nations weary themselves for nothing? For the earth will be filled with the knowledge of the glory of the Lord as the waters cover the sea" (2:12-14).

The third woe condemns Babylon's tyranny — their unrestrained exercise of power and abuse. Woe to him who builds with blood! They had forced their subjects into brutal labor to construct their kingdom. Many suffered and died so that Babylon could become greater in her own eyes. God hasn't turned a blind eye.

"Woe to him who makes his neighbors drink — you pour out your wrath and make them drunk, in order to gaze at their nakedness! You will have your fill of shame instead of glory. Drink, yourself, and show your uncircumcision! The cup in the Lord's right hand will come around to you, and utter shame will come upon your glory! The violence done to Lebanon will overwhelm you, as will the destruction of the beasts that terrified them, for the blood of man and violence to the earth, to cities and all who dwell in them" (2:15-17).

With this woe, God promises what goes around will come around! As the Babylonians had humiliated their neighbors, their reign of terror would end with their own humiliation. This is a promise of retributive judgment: what they'd done to others would come back to haunt them. The song also addresses Babylon's gods:

"What profit is an idol when its maker has shaped it, a metal image, a teacher of lies? For its maker trusts in his own creation when he makes speechless idols! Woe to him who says to a wooden thing, Awake; to a silent stone, Arise! Can this teach? Behold, it is overlaid with gold and silver, and there is no breath at all in it. But the Lord is in His holy temple; let all the earth keep silence before him" (2:18-20).

With this fifth woe, God contrasts dumb idols — carvings of wood and stone that can't speak — with people who will be dumbstruck when His glory is finally revealed. Babylon's handcrafted gods are measured against Almighty God, who handcrafted the entire universe. Checkmate!

You might look back over that entire passage and be thinking, "That's about Babylon thousands of years ago. I have no idea what that means to me." Don't worry. We're going to see that this passage is actually very, very practical for us today.

HEBREW WORD HELPS

Woe to him who *heaps up* what is not his own – for how long? (Hab. 2:6)

Original Word: רָבָה
Part of Speech: Verb
Transliteration: rabah
Phonetic Spelling: (raw-baw')
Definition: multiply

In this context: *Woe to him who is continually increasing what is not his own.*

Our day isn't so different from the days of Judah and Babylon. As people of faith, we live today among people of unfaith. We live among people who do not share or even respect our beliefs. In some instances, we live among people who actively oppose our beliefs, and may even become hostile toward us. There is a lot to be learned of our own day — the religious context we live in — by examining Judah and Babylon.

Let me show you five characteristics the Babylonians exhibit in their unrighteousness. I've touched upon them already, but with a deeper consideration I think you'll quickly recognize that they are alive and well in our day.

Filling the Void

The first characteristic, attached to that first woe in the text, is greed. Verse 6 reads, "Woe to him who heaps up what is not his own." A modern translation puts it this way: "Woe to him who piles up stolen goods and makes himself wealthy by extortion."

The Babylonians were ruthless in their greed. They ravaged neighboring countries. Why? To fill their coffers; the pursuit of riches. They are an example — there will always be those who, like them, have an insatiable appetite for more.

The Hebrew word that is translated "heaps up" adds more clarity. The word literally translates as "many." But in the Hebrew mindset, it just doesn't mean *many* as in a having a plethora of something, or an overabundance of stuff. Rather, it carries within it the concept of greed — the Babylonians were greedy, they could never have enough.

That's our world, isn't it? Our world is motivated by greed. People have an abiding sense that they don't have enough; they're never satisfied. And, so what do they do? They furiously busy themselves, attempting to gain more and more and more. Why is that? Greed is grounded in humanity's lack of self-worth. People believe that if they only had enough stuff, then other people would like them because of their things. And, if other people like them, that compensates for what really causes them to ache inside — a lack of self-worth.

But this void within us is the proverbial "bottomless pit." Try to fill it with things, and more things, and more things — it will never satisfy.

What's really missing? What's really lacking? As believers, we know the answer: God! That longing inside a man will never be satisfied by stuff! That is because, as renowned Christian philosopher Blaise Pascal asserted, "There is a God shaped vacuum in the heart of every man which cannot be filled by any created thing, but only by God, the Creator, made known through Jesus."

Jesus spoke directly to that on our behalf in the Sermon on the Mount.

"Therefore I tell you, do not be anxious about your life, what you will eat or what you will drink, nor about your body, what you will put on. Is not life more than food, and the body more than clothing? Look at the birds of the air: they neither sow nor reap nor gather into barns, and yet your heavenly Father feeds them. Are you not of more value than they? And which of you by being anxious can add a single hour to his span of life? And why are you anxious about clothing? Consider the lilies of the field, how they grow: they neither toil nor spin, yet I tell you, even Solomon in all his glory was not arrayed like one of these. But if God so clothes the grass of the field, which today is alive and tomorrow is thrown into the oven, will he not much more clothe you, O you of little faith? Therefore do not be anxious, saying, 'What shall we eat?' or 'What shall we drink?' or 'What shall we wear?' For the Gentiles seek after all these things, and your heavenly Father knows that you need them all. But seek first the kingdom of God and his righteousness, and all these things will be added to you" (Matthew 6:25-33).

For starters, did you notice that Jesus repeated one word many times over? It's the word, "anxious." Did you catch it? Six times it's used in this short passage. The original Greek word means "a sense of inner insecurity." Jesus is addressing the idea that you are insecure in your inner realm, in your inner places, and you don't understand why. To that, Jesus emphatically encourages, "Don't worry! Trust God."

Now look carefully — when you are anxious and lack trust in God, and when you are running around, pursuing things to fill the void, Jesus said, "You're acting like the Gentiles."

The Bible uses the term "Gentile" in a number of ways. It is sometimes used in a general sense for all those who are not Israelites. It is used also in referring to the people who inhabited Samaria. Sometimes the term is used to refer to a race or nation of people — the nation of Gentiles. The most predominant way it's used, however, is of a non-believer — someone who doesn't know God, doesn't trust God — a pagan or a heathen.

That's how Jesus used it here. You see, when you're filled with anxiety because of the things of the world, you're reverting back to what you used to be. You're acting like a person of non-faith. You're acting like a pagan, a heathen. That's not who we are called to be! It's as if Jesus is saying, "That inner anxiety that you never have enough, you can leave that behind because now you're a child of God — and God knows what you need."

GREEK WORD HELPS

Therefore I tell you, do not be *anxious* about your life, what you will eat or what you will drink, nor about your body, what you will put on (Matt. 6:25).

Original Word: μεριμνάω
Part of Speech: Verb
Transliteration: merimnaó
Phonetic Spelling: (mer-im-nah'-o)
Definition: abiding unsettledness; anxious about, distracted; cares.

In this context: *being deeply unsettled, abidingly anxious*

You see, the unbeliever knows nothing of the contentment we can have trusting in our Heavenly Father — relying on Him to provide. It's so easy to get caught up in that world of worry that we won't have enough. But again, that's not who we are in Christ.

Back in Habakkuk, we're given a preview of the results of living a life like that: "Will not your debtors suddenly arise?" If you're always wanting more, more, more, count on the fact that there is a payday coming. There is an end to greed.

Unfortunately, many people live out this scenario in our day and age. They strive to fill the empty void inside of them with material possessions, pushed by greed. And they find it's never enough. They continue until they get themselves into such deep financial troubles that "their debtors arise," and come after them.

But understanding why it started in the first place, we can push back. Someone once said, "We buy things we do not need with money we do not have in order to impress people we do not like." There's truth in that. So we look at that characteristic of greed in Babylon and recognize that what God is saying to Habakkuk and to the people of Judah is, "That's not you! That's not your lifestyle. That's not your path."

The next characteristic, attached to the second woe, is exploitation. Verses 9 and 10 reveal, "Woe to him who gets evil gain for his house … by cutting off many peoples." Remember that the Hebraic language is very image-oriented. God painted a picture Habakkuk would have picked up on right away.

A Babylonian man goes out to build his home on the highest hill that he can find. The problem is that it's not his hill. So he takes the hill by force. Construction can begin. But now he needs materials. He goes to someone else's forest and cuts down all their trees to supply his project. Then he determines that he needs stones. He goes to someone else's home that was built with stone, tears it down, and carts the stones off to use in his house.

What is the result of such exploitation? Verse 11 says, "For the stones will cry out from the wall, and the beams from the woodwork respond." Every time you walk into that house, the house itself testifies of your exploitation. Shame on your house! That's what the Babylonians were doing. They were exploiting their neighbors. God's word to Habakkuk and to the people of Judah is, "That's not you! That's not your lifestyle. That's not your path."

How does God feel about exploitation?

"Whoever oppresses a poor man insults his Maker, but he who is generous to the needy honors him" (Proverbs 14:31).

In our day it's the same. Chances are that when you think about exploitation today you think of politics or big business or charity fundraisers dipping their hands in the coffers. But exploitation is much simpler and closer to home than all that — it's any elevation of self over someone else.

Exploiting others isn't us! That's not our path because the very essence of our life in Christ is, out of love for Him, to be oriented selflessly toward others. As the apostle Paul exhorted:

"If there is any encouragement in Christ, any comfort from love, any participation in the Spirit, any affection and sympathy, complete my joy by being of the same mind, having the same love, being in full accord and of one mind. Do nothing from selfish ambition or conceit, but in humility count others more significant than yourselves. Let each of you look not only to his own interests, but also to the interests of others" (Philippians 2:1-4).

Our calling in Christ is to be selfless — the opposite of selfish and self-serving. But we have to be careful; we can easily slip into using others for selfish gain.

If you're an employer, be careful not to exploit your employees in your expectations of them — of the time that you require of them. If you're an employee, be careful that you do not exploit your employer — give them a full day's work. Be careful what you do with your employer's property. Don't take it home to be used in your own personal life. That's exploitation.

Husbands, we have to be careful not to exploit our wives. They've entrusted their lives and their hearts to us — we know their fears, the areas of their weakness. Wives, it's the same with your husband. Don't exploit one another's weaknesses for your own personal gain. Serve one another selflessly.

We even have to be careful not to exploit our friends. We should ask ourselves, "Are our friendships based on our giving and caring, or only on what get out of them?" It's one of the great tragedies of American friendships — many times people look for friends so that they might acquire what they have or use what they have to their advantage. Some make friends solely to join status groups that aren't their own. That's exploitation.

What is the consequence? Verse 10 says, "You have devised shame for your house."

Are you familiar with the term *shame culture*? A shame culture is a culture in which conformity of behavior is maintained through an

WHEN YOUR CIRCUMSTANCES CHALLENGE THE PROMISES OF GOD

individual's fear of being shamed.

You see a hint of it in some walks of Judaism, but it's predominantly seen in Asian cultures — people go to great lengths to avoid offending others and thereby bring shame on their family name by their actions. In those cultures, shame is a stigma that will last for generations.

Why is this important to us? We have to be careful as well, for if we exploit others, it reflects on — or shames — the name of Christ. It's not about us! Our identity in Christ is of the utmost importance.

The third characteristic, attached to the third woe of the passage, is violence. Verse 12 reads, "Woe to him who builds a town with blood and founds a city on iniquity!" This might be the most obvious hallmark of the Babylonians — they were a people who loved to shed blood. They built their empire on it.

The Hebrew word rendered "blood" in this verse is plural in form — it speaks of a continuous bloodletting. They were relentless in their

HEBREW WORD HELPS

Woe to him who builds a town with *blood* and founds a city on iniquity! (Hab. 2:12)

Original Word: דָּם
Part of Speech: Noun Masc. Plural
Transliteration: dam
Phonetic Spelling: (dawm)
Definition: bloodshed

In this context: *builds through the shedding of much blood*

violence. You may recall from earlier — back in verse 5 — that the Babylonians were described as "greedy as the grave." Their appetite for blood and death was insatiable. They could never have enough.

Historians tell us that one of the ways the Babylonians demonstrated their superiority over their captives was through public beheadings. That sounds hauntingly familiar, doesn't it? Have you caught the news lately? History repeats itself. Not to mention, the Babylonians resided in what is modern-day Iran and Iraq.

I can't overstate the importance of this: We have to be careful about exalting violence in our day. Allow me to share with you personally for a moment. Please don't hear this as some preacher's admonition toward legalism, but rather from my heart as a dad.

I believe that we, as parents, need to be careful about the violence we allow our children to be subjected to, whether in television or movies or video games.

I don't allow my son to play violent video games. Now, I used to run around with my buddies in the woods and play Rambo and war with toy weapons. I do understand a boy's proclivity toward those types of things, but I don't want to accentuate it in his mind. Because here's the tricky thing about entertainment: entertainment moves to tolerance.

When you can be entertained by something that would normally be repugnant, you've moved to tolerance. When you move to tolerance, then you move to acceptance. When you move to acceptance, then you move to action! We live in a society that has violence as a basis for much of our entertainment; it really shouldn't surprise us when it shows up in reality — and fills the headlines.

Let me challenge you to think for a moment about what you allow into your mind. What movies do you go to see? What entertains you?

Consider the words of Jesus recorded in Luke's gospel:

> "Your eye is the lamp of your body. And, when your eye is healthy, your whole body is full of light, but when it is bad your body is full of darkness. Therefore, be careful lest the light in you be darkness" (Luke 11:34-35).

That last phrase — "be careful lest the light in you be darkness" — is better understood as "lest the light *become* darkness." Please don't hear this in a legalistic way, but rather as a caution: there is a danger of progression as I've described — tolerance, acceptance, action.

When I was in college, I didn't go to movies. It wasn't a spiritual thing. It was an economic thing — you know, poor college student. I never had the money. After college, I went to seminary — and, if you thought you were poor in college, you're really poor in seminary! We had no money to go to the movies. Michelle and I probably didn't go to a theater for a good eight to 10 years.

After seminary, I went out with some friends to see a movie. It wasn't a "chick flick." It was one of those "guy movies." It was filled with violence and coarse language — stuff that I hadn't been exposed to for those eight to10 years. Seeing the movie, I got this inner sense of conflict — a great discomfort with what I was watching. I don't remember ever having experienced that before. I believe it's because I had been desensitized to it before so as not to be bothered by it. But now, separated from it for so long, it bothered me.

We are followers of Christ. Our identity is in Jesus. We should do whatever it takes to live out that identity: to avoid walking in unrighteousness, and to walk in righteousness instead. This is one of those gray areas where you will have to decide for yourself, "I'm not going to allow that into my life for the sake of Jesus Christ."

Look at what God says about violence. In verse 13 we read, "Behold, is it not from the Lord of hosts that peoples labor merely for fire, and nations weary themselves for nothing?" The Babylonians were laboring in their violence in vain. All of their conquests would soon burn up in fires. They'd wearied themselves for nothing.

In That Day

In verse 14, we get a glimpse into the glory to come: "For the earth will be filled with the knowledge of the glory of The Lord." Lest you think we'll miss it, it will be as obvious "as the waters cover the sea." God is promising, "There's going to come a day" — and this is a millennial reality — "when the Lord reigns in his Kingdom, and he will be known as the God of Peace throughout the world."

Every believing heart cries, "Come, Lord Jesus!"

6

Contrast

The contrast between Babylon and Judah, their two lifestyles or paths, is seen further in a fourth characteristic the Babylonians exhibit in their unrighteousness, attached to the fourth woe in the text — seduction.

Verse 15 reads, "Woe to him who makes his neighbors drink — you pour out your wrath and make them drunk, in order to gaze at their nakedness!" You could sum this up as seduction, which, if you think of it, follows naturally from where we've come. What goes hand in hand with greed, exploitation, and violence but seduction?

That is the historical picture we have of the Babylonians: they violently conquered their enemies and then offered them wine to intoxicate them. Once inebriated, they could easily be taken advantage of and be sexually seduced.

Earlier I mentioned what historians and archaeological finds have suggested — that Babylon was really a culture steeped in drunken debauchery.

Recall the passage we looked at in the book of Daniel that mentioned one of Balshazzar's drunken celebrations. It depicted an orgy, and in the midst of it Balshazzar ordered the slaves to go into the treasury and retrieve the gold vessels they had taken from Judah. These weren't ordinary cups, saucers, and bowls — they were sacred items, and the Babylonians defiled them by pouring wine in them and drinking from them as a part of their lewdness. We stopped right there, though, when we looked at the passage earlier. Now would be a good time to read on:

> "Immediately the fingers of a human hand appeared and wrote on the plaster of the wall of the king's palace, opposite the lampstand. And the king saw the hand as it wrote. Then the king's color changed, and his thoughts alarmed him; his limbs gave way, and his knees knocked together" (Daniel 5:5-6).

God said, "I've had enough of your excess!" It is a frightening scene. A hand appeared and began to write on the wall. Just a hand! That's got to be a quick way to ruin a good party, yes?

Just a hand shows up out of nowhere and begins to write on the wall? That would do! "Can you believe how late it's getting? I'm afraid I must go! Where's the exit?"

The passage even says, "then the king's color changed." Do you think?

When you read the text, you might say the king "couldn't read the writing on the wall" — in fact, this passage in Daniel 5 is where that popular expression originated. The story continues:

"The king called loudly to bring in the enchanters, the Chaldeans, and the astrologers. The king declared to the wise men of Babylon, 'Whoever reads this writing, and shows me its interpretation, shall be clothed with purple and have a chain of gold around his neck and shall be the third ruler in the kingdom.' Then all the king's wise men came in, but they could not read the writing or make known to the king the interpretation. Then King Belshazzar was greatly alarmed, and his color changed, and his lords were perplexed" (Daniel 5:7-9).

None of the kingdom's seers could interpret the writing on the wall. Then someone reminded the king that they held a captive named Daniel — one of the exiles from Judah. Daniel was thought to have insights into this sort of thing, so they summoned him.

Do you remember what Daniel said to the king? He said, "Wow! I'm glad I'm not you!" A loose paraphrase, of course, but he did tell the king that the kingdom would be torn from his hand and given to another. That's a rather bold statement. And it came to pass that very night! God turned the table.

That's consistent with what we see in God's answer to Habakkuk, too. In verse 15, the Babylonians are seducing those they'd conquered. In verse 16 we read, "You will have your fill of shame instead of glory! Drink yourself, and show your uncircumcision!" You will be disgraced. Judgment is coming. God will turn the table.

Next we read, "The cup in the Lord's right hand...." That phrase may sound familiar to you, especially if you've read Jeremiah, Obadiah, or the Psalms, where it appears often. What does it mean? It refers to the Lord's vengeance. God is going to have vengeance on those who treat others in this way — seducing them in order to fulfill their own sexual desires. He says specifically, the cup of the Lord's right hand "will come around to you and utter shame will come upon you."

I could leave it there and move along, or I could linger here for one more moment and show you another graphic little twist. With apologies if I spoil your appetite, let me call your attention to the word "shame" in that verse. In Hebrew, its meaning carries more than the ideas of embarrassment or humiliation we typically associate with it in English. The Hebrew word literally translates to "vomit" or "a vomit of disgrace."

Think of the context. They're drinking excessively. What happens when you drink excessively? Have you ever heard of "rebound effect"? A lot of university research has been done on this — especially in frat houses. The rebound effect is what happens when the body tries to bring itself back into balance. If you drink too much, your body

HEBREW WORD HELPS

You will have your fill of *shame* instead of glory (Hab. 2:16).

Original Word: קָלוֹן
Part of Speech: Noun Masc.
Transliteration: qalon
Phonetic Spelling: (kaw-lone')
Definition: dishonor, disgrace

In this context: *sickening embarrassment; vomit inducing disgrace*

rebounds, or vomits out what you were drinking. Aren't you glad I lingered on this point?

But hang on. There's a context to this. God says, "The excesses in your own life will come back and be shameful to you." Rebound effect.

Verse 17 says, "The violence done to Lebanon will overwhelm you." Both the Old Testament and ancient extra-biblical histories record that the Assyrians and the Babylonians employed extensive logging that essentially raped the land of its trees — a violence and seduction of the land. Why? For their own gain. Are you starting to see a pattern?

Excessive alcohol doesn't bring them joy. What does it do? It brings them misery. Sexual sin doesn't give them glory. It brings embarrassment. Their violent ways don't give them power; it brings destruction.

What can we learn from all this? If we're not careful, our selfish desires can rise to the point where we will seduce others for our own fulfillment. In this example, it's a sexual fulfillment. It's in addressing that sort of sin that the apostle Paul warned believers: run!

> Flee from sexual immorality. Every other sin a person commits is outside the body, but the sexually immoral person sins against his own body. Or do you not know that your body is a temple of the Holy Spirit within you, whom you have from God? You are not your own, for you were bought with a price. So glorify God in your body" (1 Corinthians 6:18-20).

Use the Word of God as a mirror for a moment. Is there any element of sexual seduction going on in your life for your own pleasures? As a follower of Christ, your body is a temple of the Holy Spirit — He dwells in you.

If you're not married, are you allowing your lifestyle to slip into sexual activities that belong only in the committed relationship between a man and a woman — a married relationship? If you're practicing that, scripture is very clear, "Destruction awaits you." Turn and run from it!

Married men and women, are you allowing your minds to drift into areas where you are playing with sexual fantasies? Where you're dabbling in pornography? This is not just an issue for the male population today, by the way. Studies show a big upturn in the number of women viewing pornography. This is a collective issue. It will lead to your own destruction. Turn and run!

Are you flirting with the idea of someone outside your own married relationship to fulfill your own sexual desires? Listen! It leads to destruction. We've seen it over and over again. Why is it that we don't believe it could happen to us? When you flirt with the seduction of someone else for your own sexual gain, it will always, always, always lead to your own destruction. Turn and run from it!

The last characteristic the Babylonians exhibit in their unrighteousness is found in connection with the fifth woe in the text — idolatry. Verse 18 reads, "What profit is an idol when its maker has shaped it, a metal image, a teacher of lies? For its maker trusts in his own creation when he makes speechless idols!"

It's connected to the woe in verse 19, "Woe to him who says to a wooden thing, Awake; or to a silent stone, Arise!" God is mocking the Babylonians: As if you could say anything to a stone and have it hear and respond! What foolishness!

Can it speak? Can it teach you anything? It's made of wood or stone; it's overlaid with gold or silver. A craftsman made it! It has no breath in it at all! You go right ahead and hold your breath until it speaks up, or until it gets up and does something! Anything!

The Babylonian's path was littered with idolatry. In fact, if you travel to that region of the world today, there are so many archeological digs that have produced so many ruins of small, carved idol figures that you can buy them in just about any shop. For pocket change you can fill your pockets with little gods!

The Psalmist spoke of the folly of idolatry in great clarity:

"Their idols are silver and gold, the work of human hands. They have mouths, but do not speak; eyes, but do not see. They have ears, but do not hear; noses, but do not smell. They have hands, but do not feel; feet, but do not walk; and they do not make a sound in their throat. Those who make them become like them; so do all who trust in them" (Psalm 115:4-8).

How is this relevant? Think about it. We have just as much idol worship in our culture today as Babylon ever had. We just call it by different names. People say that they're "spiritual." Have you heard that term? We don't say, "I bow down to idols." We say things like, "I'm a very spiritual person," or "I seek an inner spirituality," or "I am trying to balance the chi of life." All kinds of interesting words and terms.

Speaking of idolatry, James Montgomery Boice has postulated that it's still popular today for three reasons. First: "It offers religion without morality." That's exactly right. You can be "spiritual" and live however you want because you are the author of your own spirituality. Idols can't answer you — and you don't have to answer to them.

Secondly, Boice says: "It offers revelation without doctrine." Again, absolutely true! Idolatry has no absolutes whatsoever. If you remove the absolutes of Scripture, you can embody your own brand of revelation — whatever suits you — and live however you want. It makes everyone's revelation equal: What works for you is good for you; what works for me is good for me; and, in the end, all roads lead to … wherever all roads lead.

Thirdly, Boice says: "It offers salvation without a Savior." In other words, you become your own savior. This is the world that we live in today. Every human being can sit on the throne of his or her own life, as "spirituality" allows for that. You're the master of your soul's salvation.

So here's the reality of the world we find ourselves in: The "spiritual" world and its idolatry will push against the truth of the true God until they force those who believe in absolutes, believe in a literal Savior, and believe in the Word of God to extinction.

It should not shock us today that even the American Church is on the verge of being persecuted. Jesus warned us of this Himself:

"If the world hates you, know that it has hated me before it hated you. If you were of the world, the world would love you as its own; but because you are not of the world, but I chose you out of the world, therefore the world hates you. Remember the word that I said to you: 'A servant is not greater than his master.' If they persecuted me, they will also persecute you" (John 15:18-20).

The unbelieving world pushes against us because we stand for the one true God, the one who's represented in Habakkuk 2:20: "But the Lord is in his holy temple; let all the earth keep silence before him."

Do you see the word "but"? That's a transitional statement, "But the Lord" — and, by the way, "the Lord" there is *Yahweh*, the covenant name of God. "But the Lord is in His holy temple." He's not provoked or persuaded by their idolatry. What is His response? "Let all the earth keep silence." Why? Because we can't speak; we lack words; we are in awe of the glory of the true God.

Putting It in Perspective

Let me share two more passages of scripture to help fill out and frame the bigger picture. The first is one of the most beautiful psalms of King David — Psalm 24. It ends with a powerfully moving chorus of praise, "Lift up your heads, O gates! Be lifted up, O ancient doors, that the King of glory may come in." Please don't overlook the beginning, however — it forms the basis for that resounding praise:

> "The earth is the Lord's and the fullness thereof, the world and those who dwell therein, for he has founded it upon the seas and established it upon the rivers" (Psalm 24:1).

David makes a profound statement: Everything belongs to God! The earth? It's His. Everything that fills the earth? It all belongs to Him. Everyone who dwells on the earth? They're all His.

Consider again the characteristics of Babylon's way in light of the fact that everything belongs to God: Greed over the things that belong to God; exploitation of those who belong to God; violence toward those God loves; the seduction of others to fill a void that only God fills; idolatry or fashioning gods out of the very materials

God Himself created and owns. Talk about utter folly!

The other path — the way of contrast with the Babylonians — was Judah's. They knew better. They understood that everything they had came from the hand of God.

Do you recognize that in your own life? The things you possess aren't really yours. Your home is not yours — and I'm not talking about having a mortgage, your home doesn't even belong to the bank — it belongs to God. The car you drive is not yours. It belongs to God. You might be thinking, "I wish God would make the car payments for me!" Be of good cheer! He does! He's making them through you.

Your children belong to God! They're His, not yours. During those terrible twos, and the awkward adolescent or trying teenage years, you can legitimately cry out to God in prayer, "Will you just look at what YOUR kid is doing?!?"

The first thought that should come to mind for a believer, where all that we have is concerned, is stewardship — although we're been entrusted with these things and this place of habitation, none of it ever ceases to be God's. We're stewards of that which He has given to us for a very short period of time — like a mist is the breadth of life.

That realization brings me to the second passage I mentioned. Why is this matter of recognizing God's rightful ownership of all things and our practice of stewardship so important? This is what God says:

> "Take care lest you forget the Lord your God by not keeping his commandments and his rules and his statutes, which I command you today, lest, when you have eaten and are full and have built good houses and live in them, and when your herds and flocks multiply and your silver and gold is

multiplied and all that you have is multiplied, then your heart be lifted up, and you forget the Lord your God, who brought you out of the land of Egypt, out of the house of slavery … Beware lest you say in your heart, 'My power and the might of my hand have gotten me this wealth.' You shall remember the Lord your God, for it is he who gives you power to get wealth, that he may confirm his covenant that he swore to your fathers, as it is this day. And if you forget the Lord your God and go after other gods and serve them and worship them, I solemnly warn you today that you shall surely perish. Like the nations that the Lord makes to perish before you, so shall you perish, because you would not obey the voice of the Lord your God" (Deuteronomy 8:11-14, 17-20).

The passage offers a warning: "Lest when you have eaten … when all that you have is multiplied … your heart be lifted up and you forget the Lord your God." That's an indictment of the Babylonian path. They'd become arrogant — "Look what we've done!" And God revealed that they'd accomplished nothing but their own ruin, they just didn't know it yet.

This passage is also an indictment of the day we live in, isn't it? Our culture believes it's ours to make and ours to control. It's ours to rise up, pat ourselves on the back, and declare, "Look what I've made of myself!" Jesus spoke to this attitude:

"If anyone would come after me, let him deny himself and take up his cross and follow me. For whoever would save his life will lose it, but whoever loses his life for my sake and the gospel's will save it. For what does it profit a man to gain the whole world and forfeit his soul? For what can a man give in return for his soul? For whoever is ashamed of me and of my words in this adulterous and sinful generation, of him will the Son of Man also be ashamed when he comes in the glory of his Father with the holy angels" (Mark 8:34-38).

What does the Babylonian path profit? Where does it lead? God's answer to the prophet Habakkuk revealed the answers. History has confirmed it. That's a path you don't want to go down.

We can thank God for the contrast in Habakkuk 2 — between a lifestyle of belief and a lifestyle of unbelief. You are people of belief; you are people of faith. What's your takeaway? A look in the mirror:

The characteristics of greed, exploitation, violence, seduction, and idolatry — are there any vestiges of these whatsoever in your life? If so, eradicate them! Whatever the cost! Change your lifestyle, your habits, your actions. Those things lead you away from God, not toward Him. Take this very seriously.

You may say, "But God is a God of love, and of grace, and of forgiveness, and of mercy!" Yes, He is! For that reason, if there is any scent of these characteristics in your life, fall before your loving, graceful, forgiving, and merciful God and repent! Do what He calls you to do — what He's revealed to you here in contrasting these two paths — choose to walk the right one: The righteous shall live by their faith!

7

God Our Shelter

The righteous shall live by faith. As we turn the page and begin our look into the third chapter of Habakkuk, the prophet begins to deal with that reality — he's called to live by faith. How does he proceed? In prayer.

The entire text of Habakkuk 3 is a prayer. It's probably one of the most profound prayers recorded in the Bible. It's emotional, it's honest, transparent, poetic. You could say, "It's gritty." In other words, this is real life stuff. Habakkuk's prayer will teach you how to pray.

If you're anything like me, prayer is work; sometimes it's a struggle. I always want to learn how my prayer life can be more effectual. One of the ways I've done that through the years is simply by reading and studying the many different prayers recorded in the Bible. Let me give you a quick list of some you might look up:

The prayer of Moses — Psalm 90
The prayer of Hannah — 1 Samuel 2

The prayer of David — 2 Samuel 7
The prayer of Hezekiah — 2 Kings 19
The prayer of Ezra — Ezra 9
The prayer of Jesus — John 17
The prayer of the Disciples — Acts 4
The prayer of Paul — Ephesians 1 and 3

Let Us Pray!

Those prayers serve as models. Each one will provide you with some great insights on prayer that you can put into practice in your own prayer life — reading and studying them will be a worthwhile investment of time.

Allow me to show you what I mean. Let's take a little detour, and consider one of the prayers the apostle Paul offered, recorded in Ephesians. Do you ever struggle with, "What is it, Lord, that you would want me to say?" Have you ever wondered, "How do I go about praying for other people?" Paul teaches us how to pray for others.

Remember that Paul is writing to the church at Ephesus. It's a church he has spent time with. It's a group of people he knew intimately. It's the church that he had sent his young apprentice, Timothy, to oversee. This is the setting into which Paul writes his epistle to the Ephesians. You can sense his heart in what he says to them and how he's praying for them.

"For this reason I bow my knees before the Father, from whom every family in heaven and on earth is named, that according to the riches of his glory he may grant you to be strengthened with power through his Spirit in your inner being, so that Christ may dwell in your hearts through faith — that you, being rooted and grounded in love, may have strength to comprehend with all the saints what is the breadth and length and the height and the depth, and to know the love of Christ that surpasses knowledge, that you may be filled with all the fullness of God" (Ephesians 3:14-19).

Did you notice his posture at the start? "For this reason," he said, "I bow my knees." The apostle Paul is kneeling in prayer.

I think posture is important when we're praying. While I believe you can pray standing, sitting, prostrate (lying down) — there are many ways that you can go about praying — there is something particularly meaningful about kneeling, getting on your knees to pray. This is what the apostle was doing, and the posture he took was important enough that he mentioned it.

Kneeling demonstrates a submissive attitude. When you're kneeling before the Lord, you're communicating something with your body. I think you're communicating two things, really: You're saying, (1) "God, you are superior to me; may your will be done," and (2) "I am yielding to you." It's a humbling moment when you're all by yourself and you get down on your knees to pray. You're taking prayer seriously.

While on the topic of taking prayer seriously, have you ever asked yourself, "Why do I have to go through this exercise?" Have you ever wondered, "Does prayer really accomplish anything?" As a young man, I struggled with those questions. Believing in the sovereignty of God, I wondered, "Well, then, how do my prayers enter into this?"

I came across something tremendous in the works of a Puritan preacher named Jonathan Edwards. You may be familiar with his name for his famous sermon, "Sinners in the Hands of an Angry God." That was just one message from a lifetime of sermons and writings. This is what he wrote concerning why our prayers matter:

> "The Most High is a God that hears prayer. Though he is infinitely above all and stands in no need of creatures, yet he is graciously pleased to take a merciful notice of poor worms of the dust. He manifests and presents himself as the object of prayer, appears as sitting on a mercy seat, that men may come to him by prayer. When they stand in need of anything, he allows them to come, and ask it of him, and he is wont to hear their prayers. God in his Word hath given many promises that he will hear their prayers."

Edwards began by clarifying the relationship between God, in His splendid holiness, and man in his humble and mean estate — the "worms of the dust" description he borrowed from the biblical book of Job. Then he asserts that God *purposes and promises* to hear man's prayers.

Then Edwards asked, "Why does God require prayer in order to the bestowment of mercies?" That's a Puritan way of asking, "Why does God require prayer in order to answer it?" He goes on to answer the question:

> "It is not in order that God may be informed of our wants or desires. He is omniscient, and with respect to his knowledge, unchangeable. God never gains any knowledge by information. He knows what we want a thousand times more perfectly than we do ourselves, before we ask him."

God doesn't need our prayers to fill in blanks — He knows all. So, why then? Why pray? Edwards concluded:

> "There may be two reasons given why God requires prayer in order to the bestowment of mercy: one especially respects God, and the other respects ourselves. First, with respect to God, prayer is but a sensible acknowledgment of our dependence on him to his glory. Second, with respect to ourselves, God requires prayer of us in order to the bestowment of mercy, because it tends to prepare us for its reception."

Did you catch that? We pray to God to acknowledge our dependence upon Him and in preparation to receive His answer to those prayers. I think that's marvelous!

For the Gospel's Sake

It dovetails perfectly with what we saw in Paul's prayer in Ephesians. He began that prayer, "For this reason...." Whenever you see that phrase in the Bible, ask, "For what reason?" And then back up in the context to find the answer. When we trace back in Ephesians 3 to verse 1, guess what we find there? Another "For this reason...." Back up some more.

You'll find Paul's reasoning goes all the way back into chapter 2. From the beginning of chapter 2 through verse 13 of chapter 3, he's been talking about the Gospel. It's for the sake of the Gospel that Paul is praying! His mind is completely inundated with the good news of Jesus Christ. He returns to it over and over again. He's overflowing with the message of salvation.

Do you see what he's doing? He is praying for others because of his own salvation. Please don't miss that point! We pray as redeemed people — it's our privilege; it's an honor for us to pray for others.

It's from that place that Paul prayed, "that according to the riches of his Glory, he may grant you" — now, Paul's praying for the Ephesians — "to be strengthened with power through his Spirit in your inner being." There's the beginning of the answer to how we pray for others — we pray for their spiritual strength.

In another of Paul's epistles, one of his letters to the church at Corinth, he shared about a time when he cried out to God on his own behalf, praying for relief. God answered his prayer, saying, "My grace is sufficient for you, for my power is made perfect in weakness" (2 Corinthians 12:9). When is God strongest on our behalf? When we are weak!

Paul testified, "We don't lose heart. Though our outer self is wasting away, our inner self is being renewed day by day" (2 Corinthians 4:16). So in Ephesians 3, he prays for the spiritual strength of the believers in Ephesus, that God "may grant you to be strengthened with power through his Spirit in your inner being."

It is easy to lose heart when our outer man is wasting away. I recently had an experience with that. My doctor gave me a prescription, and the medication had an adverse effect on me physically. I noticed my heart rate was elevated. I thought it was probably the coffee I consumed that was making me a little jittery, so I didn't pay much attention to it.

When evening rolled around, I noticed it again, but figured a good night's sleep would remedy the situation. I went to bed — and woke up at 2 a.m., my heart beating at least triple its normal resting rate. I was wide awake; in fact, it felt like I was exercising. I got out of bed and walked around a bit, trying to count beats per minute with my hand. Let me tell you, it's not easy to take your own pulse at 2 a.m.!

Concerned something was wrong, I decided to wake my wife Michelle. Do you know what I said? "Now, don't worry!" Anytime you wake someone up at 2 o'clock in the morning, and begin with "Don't worry"....

Anyone who has a medical background will be horrified at the next part of my story, but I told my wife that I was going to drive myself to the emergency room. I know it's a cardinal sin, but I have a friend who is a doctor who was having heart palpitations — and he road his bicycle to the ER. I figured, "If he can do that, I can certainly drive a car." Truth be told, I didn't think I was having serious heart issues. I was confident it was a reaction to the medicine prescribed to me.

I walked into a sleepy-looking ER. No doctors or patients in sight — just a guard and one lady behind a desk. She asked, "Can I help you?"

I answered, "I think I'm having some heart problems." Let me tell you, that place lit up like a Christmas tree!

I tried to tell them I didn't think it was too serious. They didn't care what I had to say at that point. They whisked me off my feet and down a hall — they were plugging me into machines as we went. In no time at all, I was in a room, all hooked up, and they were running tests on me. Things settled down pretty quickly.

By 3 a.m., I was alone in the room. I started taking selfies — me in the ER all hooked up to machines — to send to my wife and friends. I might as well do something while I'm there, right?

Seriously, those moments in life remind us just how quickly

things can change. Many of us have had a conversation with someone one day, only to find out the next that they'd suddenly passed away. Blink of an eye — that's how fast life changes.

While I am all for praying for the outer man — for our physical health — I am convinced that's not what the majority of our prayers should be for one another. The reality is: there is a day coming when all of our hearts will stop beating, but you won't stop living. We should be praying for one another that our inner man be continually renewed — that we'd be growing in Christlikeness. That's what matters most.

It would be a terrible waste of life to spend it completely healthy outwardly, but inwardly dry like a desert. That's what Paul demonstrates — pray for one another's spiritual strength.

In verse 17, Paul says "So that...." That's known as a *hina* clause in Greek — a purpose statement. Why does he do this? He does it "so

GREEK WORD HELPS

So that Christ may *dwell* in your hearts through faith (Eph. 3:17).

> Original Word: **κατοικέω**
> Part of Speech: Verb
> Transliteration: katoikeó
> Phonetic Spelling: (kat-oy-keh'-o)
> Definition: dwell in, settle in, am established in (permanently), inhabit.

In this context: *Christ may take up permanent residence in; be at home in* that Christ may dwell in your hearts through faith."

The first reason we pray for one another is for spiritual strength. The second reason we pray for one another is for Christ's preeminence in our lives. Do you see the word "dwell" in verse 17? It is *katoikēsai* — a compound word from *kata*, which means "down," and *oikos*, which means "home." What Paul is saying is "that Christ may *be at home* in your hearts." Isn't that a wonderful way to pray for someone?

Preacher and scholar John MacArthur makes an interesting point in his commentary on this passage. He says, "Christ, when He enters us, comes to live. But, He can't live comfortably until our lives are cleansed of sin." MacArthur is making reference to the essence of Lordship in our lives. Jesus is our Lord.

So how do we pray for others? We pray that Christ would be Lord of their lives; that He would be preeminent in their lives; that He would be *katoikēsai*, at home, in their hearts.

Reading on, Paul says, "that you" — there's the continuation of the purpose clause — "being rooted and grounded in love...." There's a third reason we pray for one another: We pray for love to be manifest.

Paul introduces two metaphors in this verse. He speaks of being rooted, like a plant. He also speaks of being grounded, like a building. The Greek words rendered "rooted" and "grounded" are of the perfect tense. That paints quite a thought-provoking picture.

Imagine if you threw a pebble into a pond. The pebble would strike the water and quickly sink out of site, but the effect that it has — little ringlets drifting away so that you can continue to see the effect for quite some time — that's the sense of the perfect tense: a continuing effect.

So in this prayer, you're recognizing what has already been done — God's love has been implanted in them. Now you're praying for that love to take root and become foundational — that its effects would continue to go forth.

Paul's prayer continues, "may have strength to comprehend with all the saints what is the breadth and length and height and depth, and to know the love of Christ that surpasses knowledge...."

Do you struggle with love? I do! How can we not struggle with love? We live in a world in which people grate against us, become adversarial toward us. And what are we called to do? To love them! That's not easy. Yet Christ's love has been implanted in us. What I want is access to that love. I want to be quick to put down the sinful man and move toward the man of love! That's exactly how we should pray for one another.

"....that you may be filled with all the fullness of God." There's the fourth reason we pray for one another — that we'd experience

GREEK WORD HELPS

And to know the love of Christ that surpasses knowledge, that you may be filled with all the *fullness* of God (Eph. 3:19).

Original Word: πληρωμα, ατος, το
Part of Speech: Noun, Neuter
Transliteration: pléróma
Phonetic Spelling: (play'-ro-mah)
Definition: (a) a fill, fullness; full complement; supply (b) fullness, filling, fulfillment, completion.

In this context: *supply to full capacity; to overflowing*

the fullness of God. The Greek word translated "fullness" means abundance. The preposition "with" demonstrates that this is the goal — that we be filled with the abundance of God.

It's the goal of a Christ-follower that God be full in his or her life. And that's how we should pray for others. The next time you kneel to pray for your spouse, parent, son, daughter, or friend, pray: "Lord, I pray for their spiritual strength. Make them strong today! May they sense Christ dwelling in them, and lean toward that dwelling and listen to it! May the love of Christ be manifest in them! May the fullness of God be made known through them!"

Finally, in Ephesians, look at the doxology:

> "Now to him who is able to do far more abundantly than all
> that we ask or think, according to the power at work within us,
> to him be glory in the church and in Christ Jesus throughout
> all generations, forever and ever. Amen" (Ephesians 3:20-21).

Do you believe that? That He is able to do far more abundantly than all we ask or imagine? Pray to that end! This is how we should pray for others. It is a wonderful prayer. It's a model prayer. And if you like that, you're going to love the prayer in Habakkuk. It's time we return there.

Habakkuk 3 begins:

> "A prayer of Habakkuk the prophet, according to Shigionoth.
> O Lord, I have heard the report of you, and your work, O
> Lord, do I fear. In the midst of the years revive it; in the midst
> of the years make it known; in wrath remember mercy"
> (Habakkuk 3:1-2).

We will come back to the word "Shigionoth" a little later — it's a musical term you're going to want to become familiar with. But notice right here, at the outset, Habakkuk places himself among the dumbstruck (from 2:20), praying, "I've heard of your fame, of your deeds, God." Then he proceeds to plead: "Will you do it now, in my day?"

"God came from Teman and the Holy One from Mount Paran. His splendor covered the heavens, and the earth was full of his praise. His brightness was like the light; rays flashed from his hand; there he veiled his power. Before him went pestilence, and plague followed at his heels. He stood and measured the earth; he looked and shook the nations; then the eternal mountains were scattered; the everlasting hills sank low. His were the everlasting ways. I saw the tents of Cushan in affliction; the curtains of the land of Midian did tremble. Was your wrath against the rivers, O Lord? Was your anger against the rivers, or your indignation against the sea, when you rode on your horses, on your chariot of salvation? You stripped the sheath from your bow, calling for many arrows" (3:2-9).

Right about now you may be thinking, "Can we just go back to Ephesians? I have no idea what this guy is saying!" Fear not. He is actually giving us a wonderful model, and we'll unpack it. You're going to be able to use this — today.

Look ahead in this prayer, for a moment, to where he says, "I hear and my body trembles. My lips quiver at the sound; rottenness enters into my bones; my legs tremble beneath me" (3:16). To understand the model, first recall the situation. Remember the crisis that Habakkuk is experiencing: the Babylonians are about to invade; God is using this as a tool to refine Judah; it isn't going to stop no matter how fervently Habakkuk prays. It is fair to assume the prophet is quite anxious as he prays.

We often have this misconception that faith and fear are incompatible. It's not so. The issue isn't feelings of fear — we will have those. It's about how we deal with it. That's the issue, and that's what Habakkuk is going to teach us — how to pray in the midst of a crisis.

What this passage shows is how to deal with fear — not with worry, as we're so prone to; not through resignation or giving up; not with some mustered-up bravado, pretending it doesn't exist. Habakkuk is going to teach us how to approach crisis through prayer — three 'R' words again: he *relies* on God; he *remembers* truths about God; he *rejoices* in God.

Rely, Remember, Rejoice

Habakkuk prays like this without having any of the details. God hasn't told him how the enemy will invade, hasn't told him what to expect, hasn't told him what the outcome will be, hasn't even told Habakkuk whether or not he will survive. Nothing! Can you do that? Can you rely on God even when you have none of the details? So often we're tempted to try to manipulate things, try to control the situation.

So the first thing Habakkuk teaches us is that relying on God starts with trust. He doesn't have the answers, yet he trusts that God does.

But wait! Do you remember where he started? You can look back to chapter 1: "How long will I cry out?" "When will you hear me?" "Why are you doing this?" "Why do you sit idly by?"

Those sorts of questions sound like us! That's what we do in crisis. But between that point and now, here, in chapter 3, something has changed. He's learned how to rely on God, trusting Him without having all the details.

Habakkuk begins to remind himself about God — who He is and what He's done. This prayer opens, "I've heard of your fame and your deeds! I know who you are! I don't have all the details, but I do know this — I'm in awe of you!" The remembering leads to rejoicing. The prophet essentially worships God at the outset of this prayer; rejoicing in God's worth. Something about Habakkuk's focus has shifted.

Dr. David Martyn Lloyd-Jones, in his commentary *From Faith to Fear: Studies in the Book of Habakkuk*, addressed the prophet's change in focus: "How was Habakkuk brought to such a position? It would seem that it was when he stopped thinking of his own nation, or of the Chaldeans, and contemplated only the holiness and justice of God against the dark background of sin in the world."

Our anxieties can nearly all be traced to our persistence in looking at the immediate problems themselves, instead of looking at them in the light of God. I tell you, that last sentence is worth reading again! So long as Habakkuk looked at Israel and the Babylonians, he was troubled. When he shifted his focus to God, he returned to the realm of truth, the holiness of God, and he was able to see things in an entirely new light.

The glory of God was now his chief concern.

8

Turning To God In Uncertainty

We've seen from the outset of Habakkuk's prayer that a new perspective is dawning — from the panic and desperation of chapter 1, through the moral questions of chapter 2, he is embracing the admonition that the righteous shall live by faith. The tone has changed, it's completely different. The prophet now affirms that he is willing to rely upon God.

As we look at his prayer a little more carefully, we'll see the steps I touched upon last chapter — relying, remembering, and rejoicing — as they play out.

Recall that Habakkuk's prayer began:

"O Lord, I have heard the report of you, and your work, O Lord, do I fear. In the midst of the years revive it; in the midst of the years make it known; in wrath remember mercy" (Habakkuk 3:2).

The words "do I fear" are better translated to "I stand in awe." In other words, this is an act of worship. This is what happens when you trust God — He awes you.

This is a picture of worship through the crisis. Do moments of crisis in your life lead you to worship? Or are you so overcome that worship is the furthest thing from your mind? Habakkuk's prayer shows us that trust leads to worship.

When the prophet says, "in the midst of the years make it known; in wrath remember mercy," he's demonstrating obedience to God. He trusts. He's in awe. He's willing to be obedient through this storm. "In the midst" — you might ask, "In the midst of what?" This work of God. Habakkuk sees what he's experiencing as God's doing. And he's all in.

I Stand in Awe

This is how you know you're trusting God in the midst of a personal crisis: when you're able to say, "God, I don't want the work to end. I don't want it to stop. I don't want it to cease in my life until your good and perfect will for this is complete in me." Deep in the middle of a crisis is normally when we beg, "God, stop this! Move me out of this! I don't want to experience this any longer!" But the reality is different for a mature believer.

A mature believer looks into a crisis and says, "I am going to trust you, God, even though I don't understand how it's all going to end." Trust leads to worship. Worship leads to obedience: Lord, your will be done.

The second step we see in Habakkuk's prayer is that he remembers. The prophet reminds himself of who God is and what He's done.

We'll see it over and over as we progress through his prayer, sentence by sentence.

I can't overstate the importance of the discipline of remembering in your life. Why? Because it aligns our minds with who God is; it reminds us that He is much greater than the crisis we find ourselves in; it bolsters our faith.

As we walk through this passage we'll see the prophet remind himself of six significant events. Let's examine them one at a time.

"God came from Teman, and the Holy One from Mount Paran. His splendor covered the heavens, and the earth was full of his praise" (3:3).

Habakkuk reminds himself of God's appearance at Mt. Sinai. In order to get that out of the text, a brief geography lesson will be helpful. Teman and Paran are mountain ranges in southern Israel that border Mt. Sinai. What is Habakkuk recalling? God revealed Himself in that region to care for His people. God met Moses there to give him direction:

"On the third new moon after the people of Israel had gone out of the land of Egypt, on that day they came into the wilderness of Sinai. They set out from Rephidim and came into the wilderness of Sinai, and they encamped in the wilderness. There Israel encamped before the mountain, while Moses went up to God. The Lord called to him out of the mountain, saying, 'Thus you shall say to the house of Jacob, and tell the people of Israel: You yourselves have seen what I did to the Egyptians, and how I bore you on eagles' wings and brought you to myself. Now therefore, if you will indeed obey my voice and keep my covenant, you shall be my treasured possession among all peoples, for all the earth is mine; and you shall be to me a kingdom of priests and a holy nation. These are the words that you shall speak to the people of Israel'" (Exodus 19:1-6).

In this scene, God said, "Moses, this is what you're to say. Moses, this is what you're to do." Most importantly, He said, "Moses, this is who I am, and this is what I am going to do!"

What else did Moses receive there at Mt. Sinai? The law. This wasn't just some private consultation with Moses; this was God longing to be with His people. That's the point. This is the recollection that comforts Habakkuk. He's reminding himself of the great turning point in Israel's history — a time when God showed up powerfully and unmistakably.

Another little morsel before we move on: the word "God" in this passage is *Elohim — God the divine deliverer*. In the context of the Exodus, it's God appearing to Moses and leading His people — this is Habakkuk's takeaway: God came to them; He will come to me also.

Pause and Reflect

Let me call your attention to an unfamiliar word you'll see. It will appear a few times off to the right of the text — the word *Selah*. Scholars have concluded that it's a musical notation. If you're reading through the Psalms — the hymnal or worship manual of the Bible — you'll see this word 71 times. It's to be interpreted like a musical rest, suggesting, "Pause here for a just a moment, take a breath and reflect."

You'll notice the appearance of *Selah* at this point — right here. God is remembered as *Elohim*, coming to deliver and lead His people. This is a recollection of who God is and what He does. That is worth contemplating a while!

As an aside, *Selah* as a musical notation says something about how we should view music in relation to our worship of God. The lyrics of our music ought to move our minds. That's one of the things I love about the worship leaders at our church, The Chapel. They choose music very carefully. They're Biblio-centric about what we sing. In other words, they're theologians first, and song leaders second. That's very important. We're blessed as a congregation.

Sometimes without realizing it, we can find ourselves singing some pretty poor theology. A song might sound nice. It can make you feel good, tap your foot, or clap your hands, but if it isn't sound theologically, what are we singing? I've used the term "bubble-gum music." It tastes good. Makes you feel good. Maybe you can even blow a gigantic bubble! But it has no nutritional value whatsoever.

So having worship leaders who choose music that moves our minds in truth — *that* is a tremendous gift. Remember, when we unite our voices in song during a worship service, we're not singing for our enjoyment. We're singing of God, His attributes, His promises. There is truth in these songs worthy of reflection — *Selah!*

That's what we find Habakkuk doing here. He remembers God's appearance on Mt. Sinai. He ponders it. He continues on:

"His brightness was like the light; rays flashed from his hand; and there he veiled his power" (3:4).

Do you know what Habakkuk is reminding himself of here? The

Shekinah glory! He's thinking back upon the time when God was visibly present with His people. Do you recall what happened during the Exodus?

> "And the Lord went before them by day in a pillar of cloud to lead them along the way, and by night in a pillar of fire to give them light, that they might travel by day and by night. The pillar of cloud by day and the pillar of fire by night did not depart from before the people" (Exodus 13:21-22).

God showed up to His people as a cloud by day and a pillar of fire by night. The Shekinah glory is the visible manifestation of God before the people. Habakkuk is comforted in the recollection that God goes before, God follows behind, and God is present in the midst of His people. What a precious truth to know when you're in the middle of a crisis!

In the midst of struggle, the enemy will taunt you with questions like, "Where is your God?" The enemy wants you to believe you've been forsaken, forgotten. Evil's desire is to fan the flames of doubt and discouragement in your heart. I love the Psalms for the very reason that they remind us *where God is.*

There's a section of the book of Psalms known as "Songs of Ascent." It's Psalms 120 through 134. They're given this title because the people would sing them as they were ascending to the temple to worship. If you were in and around Jerusalem, everything moved uphill toward the temple — thus the walk really was an ascent. Take a look at one of these songs:

> "I lift up my eyes to the hills. From where does my help come?

My help comes from the Lord, who made heaven and earth. He will not let your foot be moved; he who keeps you will not slumber. Behold, he who keeps Israel will neither slumber nor sleep. The Lord is your keeper; the Lord is your shade on your right hand. The sun shall not strike you by day, nor the moon by night. The Lord will keep you from all evil; he will keep your life. The Lord will keep your going out and your coming in from this time forth and forevermore" (Psalm 121).

The Psalmist served up a reminder that God is not sleeping, but rather wide awake. He may not be answering you, but He's not dormant, He's not disengaged. No. In the midst of crisis, He will keep you. We need reminders like this when we're troubled. In moments of difficulty and discouragement, the Songs of Ascent can be a real blessing. This is what Habakkuk is doing — finding blessing and encouragement by remembering.

"Before him went pestilence, and plague followed at his heels. He stood and measured the earth; he looked and shook the nations; then the eternal mountains were scattered; the everlasting hills sank low. His were the everlasting ways" (3:5-6).

Still on the same theme, now the prophet turns to the specifics of God delivering Israel. He remembers how God forced the Egyptians to release His people. He did it through plagues; He did it by overpowering them. In Habakkuk's words, "he shook the nations." God brought the strongest nation on the earth to its knees to free His people. Habakkuk terms all of this "God's everlasting ways."

Do not fear; do not worry or be anxious. What does that do? It robs you of what you know about God. In the midst of his anxiety, his own fear, the prophet is speaking to himself as much as he's praying to God. He's preaching a message to his own heart, reminding himself of who God is and how powerful He is.

Let's get practical for a moment. When was the last time God delivered you? Perhaps it was a relational deliverance, or financial, or emotional. Maybe it was physical or spiritual. As believers in Christ, we've all got stories. If you've walked with the Lord, you've seen Him move in your life. You also know that crisis is only one telephone call away!

If you're not in crisis right now, I have good news for you — a crisis is coming! Job said that man is born for trouble just as sure as sparks fly upward.

Habakkuk prepares us for those seasons in our lives with this prayer. In the midst of it, almost like an anchor point, he's remembering God. Maybe it was 10 years ago. Maybe 30 or even 50. No matter. You go back and remember. This puts your mind right where it should be — on the power of your God, in your life.

"I saw the tents of Cushan in affliction; the curtains of the land of Midian did tremble" (3:7).

Remembering yet another scene, Cushan and Midian were neighbors of Egypt. During the Exodus, they had front-row seats. These two nations formed the sides of the Red Sea. What Habakkuk is likely calling to memory, here, is the miraculous way of deliverance — God parted the Red Sea so that Israel could cross on dry land, and then when the Egyptian army tried to follow them, God removed

His hand so the waters crashed down upon them.

As word spread concerning what God had done, the neighboring nations were panic-stricken; they trembled. Do you remember how Habakkuk began this prayer? "I have heard of your fame and of your deeds!" Indeed he had. So had the surrounding unbelieving nations! The world had heard and seen.

There's another thought-provoking image to consider. When you trust God through a crisis, the world is watching. When you turn to Him, when you trust Him, when you worship Him and obey through life's steepest challenges — those around you will take notice.

They will see how you react and they will marvel at the God you worship. Your life will become a testimony of what God is doing, of how He is moving in and through your life. You will become an instrument God uses to show the world His glory, and isn't that our prayer and earnest desire? When we pray, "Lord glorify your Son; may He be high and exalted and lifted up," isn't that what we're asking? Not ourselves, not our names, not what we do, but may you, God, be exalted and your glory be made known!

When you face crisis in your life, you don't want to rob God of His glory. How do we do that? We do that when we attempt to confront conflict the way the world would. Being consumed by anxiety and fear often gives way to anger. Endeavoring to meet it in our own strength and means — "in the flesh." Do you do that? Be careful how you walk in crisis, that God would be glorified.

When we come to verses 8 through 12, Habakkuk's prayer takes on a little different twist. He adds in a series of rhetorical questions. This is a literary device — these are questions that aren't meant to be answered, but rather to provoke further thought upon the implications.

"Was your wrath against the rivers, O Lord? Was your anger against the rivers, or your indignation against the sea, when you rode on your horses, on your chariot of salvation?" (3:8)

With these questions Habakkuk is likely recalling three different events — each of which demonstrates God's supreme power. Scholars have suggested the "wrath against the rivers" refers to the Nile, and God's turning the water to blood recorded in Exodus 7. The second "anger against the river" is thought to refer to Joshua 3, and the splitting of the River Jordan. The last mention, "indignation against the sea," seems most likely a fit for the Red Sea parting. So, the questions invite: Think on this!

The next phrase in the prayer provides a poetic picture:

"You stripped the sheath from your bow, calling for many arrows" (3:9).

Think carefully about that sentence. What does an archer do when he takes his arrow and stretches back his bow? He holds life in the balance. He is able to either take a life or grant it in that very moment. This is what the prophet is recalling: God holds life in His hands; He has the authority to take life or grant life.

It goes back to power — God's got it. There's another *Selah* out to the right. This is another great place to pause and ponder for a moment.

"The mountains saw you and writhed; the raging waters swept on; the deep gave forth its voice; it lifted its hands on high. The sun and moon stood still in their place at the light of your arrows as they sped, at the flash of your glittering spear" (3:10-11).

Here the prayer of Habakkuk takes yet another step — he personifies creation and nature. The mountains react to God's splendor. The waters, too. The deep sang forth and lifted its hands. They're all responding to God as if they have a voice, as if they have hands and the volition to praise. Who has that kind of power — to bring creation to worship? Your God does!

What have we learned from Scripture? We've learned that if we don't cry out in praise and worship, the rocks will. The environment, the created earth itself, will come alive to declare His worth.

The sun, moon, and stars magnify His glory. Habakkuk speaks of a time when they stood still at God's command. He's likely recalling a time when Joshua prayed that God would make the sun stand still — extend daylight — so that Israel could vanquish its enemies. The event is recorded in the book of Joshua:

> "At that time Joshua spoke to the Lord in the day when the Lord gave the Amorites over to the sons of Israel, and he said in the sight of Israel, 'Sun, stand still at Gibeon, and moon, in the Valley of Aijalon.' And the sun stood still, and the moon stopped, until the nation took vengeance on their enemies" (Joshua 10:12-13).

The idea that you and I serve a God with such great power has to encourage our hearts in the face of whatever adversity or uncertainty that may befall us. But Habakkuk is not done yet. He rehearses a blow-by-blow account of God's shock and awe:

> "You marched through the earth in fury; you threshed the nations in anger. You went out for the salvation of your

people, for the salvation of your anointed. You crushed the head of the house of the wicked, laying him bare from thigh to neck" (3:12-13).

There's another *Selah* here too. Stop a moment! Are you taking this all in? This is your God that you're remembering! Habakkuk ponders this, and then moves on:

"You pierced with his own arrows the heads of his warriors, who came like a whirlwind to scatter me, rejoicing as if to devour the poor in secret. You trampled the sea with your horses, the surging of mighty waters" (3:14-15).

It's back to the central theme: God delivered His people. God accompanies His people. God is powerful on behalf of His people!

Why does Habakkuk do this? Why does he remind himself — and us — of all these demonstrations of God's power? Because when you are in a crisis you feel powerless!

You see how to use the Word of God in this example — how to use it in your own life. You see how to use it in your own prayer. *Selah!* Stop and ponder the amazing God you serve! Go back through your own life, like a song, and remember the moments you've lived through that were most difficult. Write it down. Pray through it. Recall all the times God has shown Himself in your life.

All of those instances when He's shown up, all those instances where He's fulfilled His promises, all those instances when He's demonstrated His power and glory — why is it important for you do this? So that you can end up where Habakkuk did — rejoicing!

Joy Has the Last Word

Habakkuk's prayer culminates in some of the greatest words — and the greatest resolve — found in all of Scripture:

"Though the fig tree should not blossom, nor fruit be on the vines, the produce of the olive fail and the fields yield no food, the flock be cut off from the fold and there be no herd in the stalls, yet I will rejoice in the Lord; I will take joy in the God of my salvation" (3:17-18).

Habakkuk concludes that even if the trees fail, the crops fail, the vines fail, the fields fail, the flock and the herds are lost (so thorough a list represents losing everything, and it's spoken as if the prophet expects it very well may happen), yet ... even so, he's going to rejoice in God!

"Yet" is a great word! Consider that this is probably the greatest transition in the entire book, and it's found in that one little three-letter conjunction. Even though my world crumbles down around me, yet I will rejoice. It's resolve: I am going to rejoice in the God of my salvation. I know Him to be worthy of my praise and the source of my joy. I know Him to be my strength. I know Him to be present with me. Look at the prayer's final declaration:

"God, the Lord, is my strength; he makes my feet like the deer's; he makes me tread on my high places" (3:19a).

But here is the thing: You can't get to this last step — rejoicing —

without going through the first two, relying on God and remembering who He is and what He's done.

Are you there? Can you rejoice? You say, "I don't know. I don't think I can rejoice in the midst of what I'm going through." Back up. Work through your reliance upon God and your remembrance of Him. Understand that this is moving you toward a realization of just who is in control of your life. When you better understand it, then you'll be able to be obedient to it — and on your knees — and say, "Yet I'll rejoice in you, God."

There's one more observation to make before we close the book. Please don't miss that Habakkuk ends with a postscript of sorts:

"To the choirmaster: with stringed instruments" (3:19b).

Habakkuk's prayer ends with an instruction that it is to be used as a worship song, committed to the choir master and accompanied by stringed instruments. It means that the prophet understood others would benefit from his experience. Pass this testimony on, in other words, believers need this!

Do you remember back in chapter 7, when we began looking at Habakkuk's prayer, that it began, "A prayer of Habakkuk the prophet, according to Shigionoth"?

I pointed out that the word *Shigionoth* is believed by scholars to be a musical term. And I promised that I'd come back to it. Here's the rest of the story:

Those same scholars believe it means that this prayer should be accompanied (are you ready for this?) "by wild, enthusiastic, and victorious music."

When your circumstances seem to challenge the very promises

of God — when the wheels appear to be falling off your world — when you're shaken by what's unfolding — the righteous shall live by faith!

Beloved, there is no other path than this. You can fight against it. You can try to work your way out of it. You can deny it. But unless and until you can bend your knees, rely on Him, remember who He is and what He's done — until those things happen — you'll not be rejoicing.

But when you do — when you walk the path Habakkuk chose — you'll be overwhelmed with an emotion you can't even begin to fathom … joy! That joy will rise to wild, enthusiastic, victorious song in your heart! It will be joy of the Spirit and of your inner being, brought to you not by your *own* doings, but by your great, powerful, loving — and ever-present — God.

BIBLIOGRAPHY

The Holy Bible: English Standard Version. (2001). Wheaton: Standard Bible Society.

Boice, J. M. (2002). *The Minor Prophets: an expositional commentary* (p. 390). Grand Rapids, MI: Baker Books

Clark, D. J., & Hatton, H. A. (1989). *A translator's handbook on the book of Habakkuk* (p. 83). New York: United Bible Societies.

Pusey, E. B. (1885). *Notes on the Old Testament: The Minor Prophets: Micah to Malachi* (Vol. 2, p. 179). New York: Funk and Wagnalls.

Smith, R. L. (1998). *Micah–Malachi* (Vol. 32, p. 99). Dallas: Word, Incorporated.

Lange, J. P., Schaff, P., Kleinert, P., & Elliott, C. (2008). *A commentary on the Holy Scriptures: Habakkuk* (pp. 12–13). Bellingham, WA: Logos Bible Software.

The Holy Bible: English Standard Version. (2001). Wheaton: Standard Bible Society.

Boice, J. M. (2002). *The Minor Prophets: an expositional commentary* (p. 390). Grand Rapids, MI: Baker Books

Clark, D. J., & Hatton, H. A. (1989). *A translator's handbook on the book of Habakkuk* (p. 83). New York: United Bible Societies.

Pusey, E. B. (1885). *Notes on the Old Testament: The Minor Prophets: Micah to Malachi* (Vol. 2, p. 179). New York: Funk and Wagnalls.

Smith, R. L. (1998). *Micah–Malachi* (Vol. 32, p. 99). Dallas: Word, Incorporated.

Lange, J. P., Schaff, P., Kleinert, P., & Elliott, C. (2008). *A commentary on the Holy Scriptures: Habakkuk* (pp. 12–13). Bellingham, WA: Logos Bible Software.

The Holy Bible: English Standard Version. (2001). Wheaton: Standard Bible Society.

Boice, J. M. (2002). *The Minor Prophets: an expositional commentary* (p. 409). Grand Rapids, MI: Baker Books

Smith, R. L. (1998). *Micah–Malachi* (Vol. 32, p. 107). Dallas: Word, Incorporated.

Sproul, R.C. (2000) *The Holiness of God, The Insanity of Luther* (p.220). Tyndale House Publishing.

Bainton, R. H. (2013) *Here I Stand: A life of Martin Luther.* Abingdon Press.

Luther. Dir. Eric Till. Perf. Joseph Fienes, Alfred Molina, Jonthan Firth, Clair Cox. MGM Films, 2003. DVD.

The Holy Bible: English Standard Version. (2001). Wheaton: Standard Bible Society.

Boice, J. M. (2002). *The Minor Prophets: an expositional commentary* (p. 410-411). Grand Rapids, MI: Baker Books

Clark, D. J., & Hatton, H. A. (1989). *A translator's handbook on the book of Habakkuk* (p. 92). New York: United Bible Societies.

Louw, J. P., & Nida, E. A. (1996). *Greek-English lexicon of the New Testament: based on semantic domains.* New York: United Bible Societies.

MacArthur, J. F., Jr. (1983). *Galatians* (p. 84). Chicago: Moody Press.

The Holy Bible: English Standard Version. (2001). Wheaton: Standard Bible Society.

Boice, J. M. (2002). *The Minor Prophets: an expositional commentary* (p. 415). Grand Rapids, MI: Baker Books

Clark, D. J., & Hatton, H. A. (1989). *A translator's handbook on the book of Habakkuk* (pp. 105–110). New York: United Bible Societies.

Strong, J. (2001). *Enhanced Strong's Lexicon*. Bellingham, WA: Logos Bible Software.

Zodhiates, S. (2000). *The complete word study dictionary: New Testament*. Chattanooga, TN: AMG Publishers.

The Holy Bible: English Standard Version. (2001). Wheaton: Standard Bible Society.

Boice, J. M. (2002). *The Minor Prophets: an expositional commentary* (p. 420-22). Grand Rapids, MI: Baker Books.

Clark, D. J., & Hatton, H. A. (1989). *A translator's handbook on the book of Habakkuk* (pp. 107–115). New York: United Bible Societies.

Jonathan Edwards. (1952). *The Works of Jonathan Edwards. Volume 2* (p. 114-116). New York: Hendrickson Publishing.

Lange, J. P., Schaff, P., Kleinert, P., & Elliott, C. (2008). *A commentary on the Holy Scriptures: Habakkuk* (p. 34). Bellingham, WA: Logos Bible Software.

Lloyd-Jones, David Martyn (1982). *From Fear to Faith, Studies in the Book of Habakkuk*. (p. 59-60). Grand Rapids, MI: Baker Books.

Strong, J. (2001). *Enhanced Strong's Lexicon*. Bellingham, WA: Logos Bible Software.

Zodhiates, S. (2000). *The complete word study dictionary: New Testament*. Chattanooga, TN: AMG Publishers.

The Genealogy of the Kings of Ancient Israel and Judah

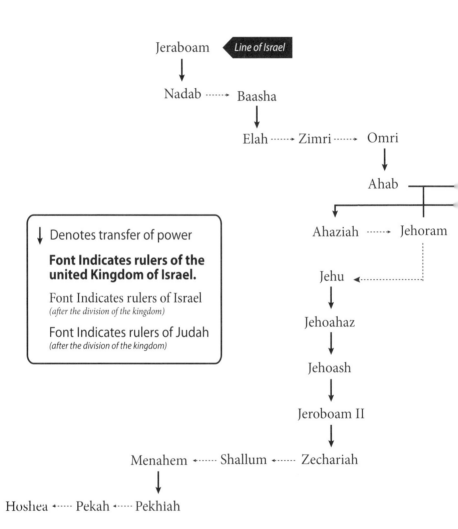

Jeraboam — **Line of Israel**

Nadab ·······▸ Baasha

Elah ·······▸ Zimri ·······▸ Omri

Ahab

Ahaziah ·······▸ Jehoram

Jehu ◂·············

Jehoahaz

Jehoash

Jeroboam II

Menahem ◂······ Shallum ◂······ Zechariah

Hoshea ◂······ Pekah ◂······ Pekhiah

↓ Denotes transfer of power

Font Indicates rulers of the united Kingdom of Israel.

Font Indicates rulers of Israel
(after the division of the kingdom)

Font Indicates rulers of Judah
(after the division of the kingdom)

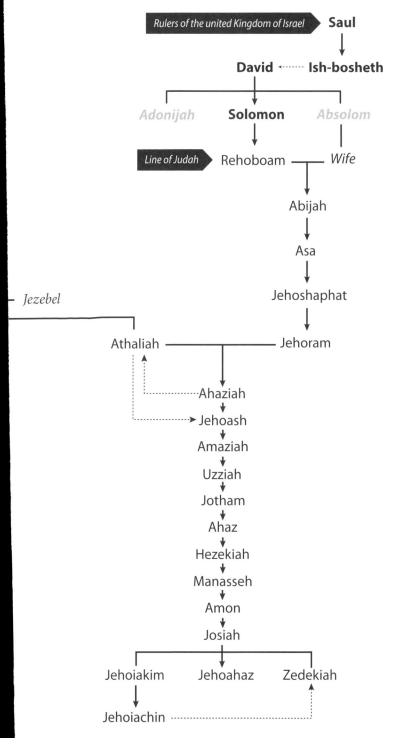

Rulers of the united Kingdom of Israel **Saul**

David ⤺······ **Ish-bosheth**

Adonijah   **Solomon**   *Absolom*

Line of Judah Rehoboam —— *Wife*

Abijah

Asa

Jehoshaphat

— *Jezebel*

Athaliah —————— Jehoram

Ahaziah

Jehoash

Amaziah

Uzziah

Jotham

Ahaz

Hezekiah

Manasseh

Amon

Josiah

Jehoiakim   Jehoahaz   Zedekiah

Jehoiachin

143